M000031043

Tanya and Raquelle have cracked the code to finding true peace, joy, and happiness every day. *The Sunshine Mind* gives readers practical daily steps to improve their mood and attitude. This is a must-read for anyone looking to become more optimistic and hopeful.

DEVON FRANKLIN, *New York Times* bestselling
author and Hollywood producer

Tanya Rad is forever a romantic of life, and this is what we need more of in the world—to see life through a never-ending lens of hope. Tanya and Raquelle have authentically and vulnerably crafted a book that will help us in our journeys to loving ourselves and in turn the world around us.

PATTY RODRIGUEZ, author, producer,
and cofounder of Lil' Libros

The Sunshine Mind is a must-read for anyone looking to incorporate mindfulness into their lives. Inspirational, empowering, and uplifting, *The Sunshine Mind* is a triumph in helping guide its readers on how to navigate the human condition.

ALEEN KESHISHIAN, founder and CEO
of Lighthouse Management + Media

For those of us lucky enough to know and love Tanya, there is one truth we know for certain: she is sunshine. In *The Sunshine Mind*, Tanya and Raquelle inspire us to live a life filled with hope: The kind of hope that strengthens. The kind of hope that shines beautiful light into every second of every day. May we all carry sunshine in our hearts and choose to see life through hope-colored glasses.

SOFIA CARSON, actor, singer, producer,
and UNICEF ambassador

THE SUN SHINE MIND

100 Days to Finding the Hope and Joy You Want

THE SUN SHINE MIND

TANYA RAD & RAQUELLE STEVENS

WITH ALLIE KINGSLEY BAKER

ZONDERVAN BOOKS

ZONDERVAN BOOKS

The Sunshine Mind
Copyright © 2023 by Tanya Rad and Raquelle Stevens

Requests for information should be addressed to:
Zondervan, *3900 Sparks Dr. SE, Grand Rapids, Michigan 49546*

Zondervan titles may be purchased in bulk for educational, business, fundraising, or sales promotional use. For information, please email SpecialMarkets@Zondervan.com.

ISBN 978-0-310-36618-8 (hardcover)
ISBN 978-0-310-36622-5 (audio)
ISBN 978-0-310-36620-1 (ebook)

Cover design: Faceout Studio, Amanda Hudson
Cover illustrations: Malte Mueller / Getty Images; Aanush / Shutterstock
Interior design: Denise Froehlich

Printed in the United States of America

22 23 24 25 26 27 28 29 30 31 32 33   /LSC/   15 14 13 12 11 10 9 8 7 6 5 4 3 2 1

CONTENTS

FOREWORD

Selena Gomez

I am so proud of Raquelle and Tanya for writing this book.

Raquelle is like my sister and has been one of my closest friends for over a decade now. I can't think of a single word that would describe her better than *bright*. When it comes to light, optimism, and appreciating all that is good in our lives, there is no one better to have by your side than Raquelle. She is the person you call when you are worried, hurt, or scared. She is the one you call when something has fallen apart entirely and you can't seem to pick yourself back up. She is always right there to offer hope and perspective. She will hand you a little joy, happily. This joy is not flimsy. It's not an empty optimism that promises everything will become better right away, but an optimism that is grounded in truth. Raquelle has helped me through some of my own hardest times.

When it comes to a partner for this book, I cannot think of a better person than Tanya. She is another friend who continues to fight for the good and believe for better times ahead. Both Raquelle and Tanya are a gift to those who know them. They are a gift to this city we call home, and I think these words they have chosen to share will be a gift to you.

It is easy to look out at the world around us and get discouraged. So many things feel broken. So many things feel beyond repair. And yet there is still the choice to show up and believe that things could be a little bit better tomorrow. Raquelle and Tanya are committed to this. While life is both good and hard, they choose hope. They choose trust. They choose grace and forgiveness and show up for people in a way that makes a difference. This is so much of what it looks like to live a life that is bright. We can walk through these days choosing to give more than we take. We can look for ways to listen and love and care. We can choose to show up and serve long after it feels easy. We can choose to let the challenging things stretch us into who we want to become, and we can choose gratitude for every single good thing we are given. I have watched Raquelle and Tanya live every bit of this out. They are strong and resilient and lighthearted through every season.

I hope the words of this book bring you comfort and perspective. I hope they leave you encouraged, and I hope they leave you feeling a little less alone. Because the truth is that every last one of us needs to be picked back up along the way. We all have moments of feeling tired or worn down or overwhelmed. May these words be like the many conversations I've had with these two friends. May they remind you that you carry everything you need to walk through the very season you are in. May they remind you that joy is one of the greatest gifts we can carry with us. It's a strength that lifts and lightens us in the middle of days that are almost always both good and challenging.

I think we all hope to live a generous life that matters to those around us. And while there are plenty of ways to do that, I can't think of anything better to bring than joy. I can't think of anything more necessary or needed in these very days than hope. So I hope that the courage, the unshaken hope, and the sunshiny joy of these two friends of mine rub off on you as you read these words they have shared.

May this book meet you right where you are and lift you up a little. This is what they have both done for me in so many moments, and I know their words can do the very same for you.

INTRODUCING

Tanya

My name is Tanya, and I'm a modern woman. I march to the beat of my own drum. I am annoyingly optimistic. I give people the benefit of the doubt. I sing out loud when I go on runs (yes, I'm *that* person). I watch rom-coms on the daily. I'm a hopeful romantic. And my relationships are everything to me. The top questions I am always asked are, "How are you always so happy?" and "How do you stay so positive?" The truth is, I'm not always, but that can be our little secret. I try to keep it real, and I exude happiness and positivity by choice and am able to maintain both because I am deeply rooted in my faith.

In my twenties I experienced a major heartbreak and felt enormous rejection. Little did I know I was being redirected to an even greater calling and destiny than the one I had imagined for myself. When I was laid off from my first job in radio, I doubted my abilities and felt terribly lost and hopeless. But a force much bigger than my own was pushing me out of a situation I now realize I would never have left on my own. I didn't know then that I was meant to be in a bigger city, with a bigger platform. It's experiences like these that remind me there's always a plan, even when you can't see it. I've seen God work in beautiful ways in my life, and it's always changed me for the better, from the inside out.

My faith wasn't always this way. I was raised in the Serbian Orthodox Church. Being part of that church was more of a Sunday formality than an internal experience or connection. I didn't truly find my faith until my early twenties. I hate to admit this, but that major heartbreak is what brought me to my knees and ultimately landed me in a Bible study.

I'm a bleeding heart. I wear my soul on my sleeve. All I ever wanted in life was to get married and have babies. So when the one relationship I'd put all those expectations on came crashing down, I was left sleepless, hopeless, confused, weak, and majorly codependent on others. I didn't know who Tanya was, what she wanted in life, or even what she did for fun. I was a shell of a woman, and as hard as it is to admit, it took me feeling this low to become the strong, independent, self-sufficient, modern woman I am today.

As I mentioned, this breakup left me on the floor. I was a cliché of a woman scorned. I went to too many parties. I was intimate with too many guys. I watched all the sad movies and ate way too much ice cream. Spoiler alert: None of it helped—not even a little. One day at work, I was crying in the hallway (which was a daily ritual for me at that point) when a friend of mine, Jason Kennedy, who was hosting for E! News at the time, saw me. He didn't know what was going on or why I was crying, but he came over to say he was sorry for whatever I was going through and asked if I'd like to come to his Bible study that night.

My mind raced. Bible study? He offered me Bible study? Not a good-looking single friend to set me up with but . . . Bible study? At that point I had tried everything else, so I figured why not give this a try? Plus, I was out of ice cream. So that night I went to Bible study. I sat in the middle row, far to the left, and was moved to tears. It was as if the pastor knew exactly what to say to make me feel less alone. For the first time in months, I finally felt like myself again.

One of the friends I met that night—Raquelle Stevens, the coauthor of this book—is like my sister now. She was happy, self-assured, secure, and deeply rooted, which I so desperately wanted to be. She was—and is—sunshine in human form. Little did I know that night, she would be a rock in my life, helping me navigate personalities, egos, contracts—you name it. The entertainment industry is not for the faint of heart, and Raquelle has talked me through every single argument, squabble, or moment of self-doubt I've had in my career while also helping me continue to shine my light.

I hope *The Sunshine Mind* is a lifesaver for you. I hope it brings you steadiness. I pray it restores hope in your heart in the places where you may have lost it. I pray that this book—and the sunshine mindset—creates a beautiful community of people who want to live life through hope-colored glasses.

Enjoy!

Tanya

INTRODUCING

Raquelle

I remember meeting Tanya Rad at her first night of Bible study like it was yesterday. Even though I had grown up in church, the Bible study Jason Kennedy had started was a special place for me. I had recently moved to LA from Chicago, and I was lonely. Shortly after moving, I had prayed, "God, if LA is where I'm meant to be, I pray that I would make the best friends I've ever made in my life and that you would make this clear to me, or I'm moving back to Chicago." I gave myself a one-year timeline, and a few months after I said that prayer, I walked into Bible study and met Tanya. I instantly knew she was one of those friends I had prayed for.

After we met, we made plans for lunch, and it was then that she opened up about the challenges she was having at work—people saying she was too positive, too nice, and that she would never make it in this industry because people never get to the top being that way. My advice to her was to keep being herself because that's exactly why God had given her that position—to spread her light and positivity, to be different in an industry that can sometimes be toxic.

Through our friendship and our shared spirituality, no matter how hard life got, Tanya always stayed true to who she is, and that is something I admire and respect. Now, after almost nine years of friendship, I have seen her year after year continually choose the high road, and I am so proud of the woman she has become. The light she gives out on television, the radio, her podcast, and social media is truly remarkable. I believe God has honored her efforts to stay true to herself because that's exactly who he created her to be, and I'm so grateful to be her friend.

When Tanya approached me about writing this book together, I thought of how beautiful it is that our faith journeys have led both of us here. As we were coming up with a title for this book, something that resonated with both of us was the word *sunshine*. With both of us being eternal optimists, people often assume life is easy for us—that we wake up happy every morning—but that couldn't be further from the truth. Like everyone else, we face challenges and hard times, which affect us deeply.

I truly love God, love life, and love people. My greatest desire has always been, and always will be, to spread God's love to people and, in return, to see people live free. Most of all, I want to help you shine to your fullest potential.

I am truly honored that you've picked up *The Sunshine Mind*, and it's my hope and prayer that you will find freedom, love, and light in the best thing I have ever known and will ever know—a relationship with God.

ACKNOWLEDGMENTS

We have so many people to thank for helping bring this devotional to life—it was a giant combination of people being generous with their connections, resources, and time. We could not have done this without every single one of you.

First we'd like to thank Erika Munger (scrub sisters for life) for connecting us to our publisher, Zondervan. You were the spark that got this fire going.

To our entire team at Zondervan—Carolyn McCready (our fearless leader), Alicia Kasen, Paul Fisher, Sarah Falter, Matt Bray, Devin Duke, Kim Tanner, Brenda Snodderly, and Bridgette Brooks: We could not have done this without you. Thank you for seeing our heart, passion, and vision for this project.

To Allie Kingsley Baker, our right hand on this project: You are the Sunshine Mind in human form; working with you on this was truly a blessing. We would have been lost without you. Thank you for believing in us. Thank you for not only your time, effort, and energy but also your leadership and knowledge in this literary world we were navigating for the first time. (And hopefully on future ones to come.)

To Roby, our "agent" on this deal (and Tanya's better half): Thank you for your time and energy and being our legal eyes on the details. Roby, you have been my greatest gift; I am so lucky to do life with you by my side. I love you so much!—Tanya

To Ashley Cook: We couldn't have done this without you!

To our parents, Sam, Branko, Dusanka & Heidi: We are forever grateful for your unwavering and unconditional love and support.

To every single person that listens to the morning show, or *Scrubbing In*, or follows us on social media: Thank you for being a part of this journey with us. Your constant encouragement has lit us up from the inside out . . . this book is for all of you!

INTRODUCTION

We're so glad you're here with us to learn about and share in our mind-set, the Sunshine Mind. We see this mindset as a daily practice. It's not a formula or a quick fix, but rather the way you go about your life each day, one day at a time. We all know life can throw us a mean curveball. Facing challenges is part of the human experience. As you read through this devotional, we hope your faith is strengthened each day and you are able to navigate life's obstacles with positivity, grace, and light. Because living life with a sunshine mindset means exuding light, positivity, and promise. *The Sunshine Mind* will restore your hope, give you practical ways to deal with the stresses that come with this digital age, and help you shine from the inside out.

We knew this book was necessary because we listened to you, whether it was those of you who messaged us on social media or walked right up to us while we were out and about, asking for better ways to conquer anxiety, overcome stress, or become stronger than the pressures of trying to live up to the world's expectations. We read and took to heart the brave comments left on our pages about needing strength to cope with the disappointments of life and wanting to discover real peace and joy. You—our listeners, followers, and friends—were the inspiration for this project. Our hope is that you feel encouraged and inspired. Let us, two girls who have been there and done that, be your gentle reminder to listen to God, pursue your passions, and spread God's love and positivity to the people around you. Remember, they're lucky to be in your presence, as are we.

TRUST GOD'S PLANS

"I know the plans I have for you," declares the Lord, "plans to prosper you and not to harm you, plans to give you hope and a future."

—JEREMIAH 29:11

Tanya

It was my senior year of college, and I was living my best life in a house with seven of my best friends and sorority sisters. (Go, Theta!) I was working my dream job as a morning show producer at a local radio station while participating in a senior honors program I'd worked hard to get into. My daily existence was the epitome of work hard, play hard—waking up before the sun to produce my awesome morning show, taking classes during the afternoon, and dashing from day to date in the evening. Life was fast and fun at twenty-one! But I'll never forget the day the fun rug was pulled out from under my feet. It started like any normal workday, except there was a weird energy in the building. Something felt off. And boy, was it! It was on that day, two weeks before my college graduation, that I was let go from my coveted position at the morning show.

I took being let go very personally. What had I done wrong? How could this have happened? Even after I was assured that this was a companywide decision and most part-time positions had been eliminated, I still didn't believe it. It *must* have been something I'd done. My mind spun as a dark cloud of self-doubt came over me. I told myself I hadn't been good enough to keep my first real job. If I had been better, this wouldn't have happened. This, of course, was before I'd found my relationship with Jesus. Yet years before I even knew who God was, here he was pushing me out of a space that was too small for me. You see, what I didn't realize at the time was that God had bigger plans for my career. He wanted me to have a greater opportunity and a bigger platform. My postcollege plan had been to stay in Tucson, Arizona, where I was comfortable, and not push myself further. So God said, "Let me help you out here, Tanya. I'm going to gently push you out of this position so you can find your own voice and a greater calling right where I want you." This calling was in Los Angeles, at a top radio market with one of the biggest shows in the country. What I didn't realize at the time of being let go—after which I'd spend many hours, days, and nights self-analyzing, second-guessing, moping, and crying—was that this setback was actually a step *forward*—a blessing from God, who was telling me, "I have bigger plans for you. Trust me."

Tanya speaking . . . I know it can be difficult in the moment (trust me, I've dealt with a lot of rejection in my life, both personally and professionally), but think of rejection as redirection from God. When a door closes, God is calling you in a different direction. The road to success will be bumpy at times, but with God as your safety belt, the destination will be worth it.

In moments of rejection, I find it helpful to write myself letters. I write a letter to my future self when I experience this rejection professionally. And I write a letter to my future husband when the rejection deals with matters of the heart. I write about the hurt and disappointment I feel in that exact moment but end the letter with a message of hope, knowing that God sees the bigger picture and will fulfill the desires of my heart because he placed them there.

Plus, the letters are something fun to look at January 1 of every year to see the progress I've made (and the love letters to the person you haven't even met yet could be a nice little treat to give to your future spouse one day!).

SHOWCASE YOUR ACHIEVEMENTS. Frame and
display your diploma, certification, or any other
accomplishment you worked hard for. Don't let an
award collect dust in a dark closet. Put that baby on a
prominent shelf!

JOURNAL. Putting thoughts on paper can give you some
aha moments.

TALK TO FRIENDS WHO SHARE YOUR FAITH. When you
connect with people who come from the same place
spiritually, you're able to meet each other on a deeper,
more meaningful level.

PRAY EVERY DAY. Keep the faith by remaining consistent
in your relationship with God.

LISTEN TO GOD. Follow the breadcrumbs set out for you.

HOLD ON TO HOPE

May the God of hope fill you with all joy and peace as you trust in him, so that you may overflow with hope by the power of the Holy Spirit.

–ROMANS 15:13

Tanya

I went through a phase of dating where I kept meeting wrong guy after wrong guy. I will spare you the details, but man, I felt like I was put through the wringer. I found myself questioning God daily: *Why, God? Are there* any *decent men left out there? Why are you testing me like this?* Until one day my hope was restored—in the form of a man. He was loving. He was kind. He was faith-filled. He was fun. He was easy on the eyes (I know, I know—this isn't the most important thing, but it doesn't hurt). He was sent from God to restore my hope. Even though the relationship didn't work out, I chose to see this experience from the bright side. It was a sign of hope from Jesus. It was his answer to all the questions I'd cried out to him. God showed me that good men do exist. He reminded me that there are men with great character and integrity in this city. He restored my faith in love. He restored my faith on my love journey.

I was dating this guy when Kacey Musgraves was in her prime. I'm talking Grammy-sweep-momentum Kacey Musgraves era. My song with this guy was Kacey's "Butterflies." I took that image—a butterfly—and made it my symbol of hope in love. Since then, every time a butterfly crosses my path, I see it as a God-wink, God putting that symbol of hope directly in my path to make sure my heart is never depleted of hope again.

If you lose your positive outlook, God can restore your hope. Think of a time when you had to trust God for something. Hopefully you were able to trust and hope because you believe God is a good God and that he's faithful and reliable even when circumstances aren't. That's ultimately what hope is—a trust that all will be well eventually. Look at your history and see how God's been faithful in the past. Use these reminders to help you continue to trust the God of hope.

THE SUNSHINE MIND WAY
TO ... HOLD ON TO HOPE

For Tanya, butterflies are visual confirmation that hope is alive. Find your butterfly today. What is that symbol in your life? Something that pops up in moments when you need your hope restored. Figure out what that symbol is and hold it close, knowing that every time you see it, God is saying, "Keep hope in your heart." You will be surprised by what having this little symbol can do for your heart.

KNOW YOUR OWN WORTH

The Spirit God gave us does not make us timid, but gives us power, love and self-discipline.

—2 TIMOTHY 1:7

Raquelle

I used to think that if I worked hard enough and was kind enough, people would notice my worth and give me the position or salary I deserved. It took me a long time to realize that unless we speak up, most people will assume we are content with whatever they offer. A few years ago I was working on a project that had been ongoing, and as the project grew, my responsibilities had grown too. But I was still making the same amount. No one was trying to take advantage of me, that's just the way the project was set up. I knew the budget was there, so I decided to call the head of the project and ask for a raise. She said of course and agreed that my pay should increase. It was a phone call I was nervous to make; asking for something often makes us feel vulnerable, even when we know it's the right thing to do. But we never get what we don't ask for, and often people are simply focused on their own jobs and responsibilities. Unless we speak up, people will assume all is well. This process took me years to learn and put into practice. It wasn't until I knew my worth that I felt ready to ask for what I wanted—and deserved.

You're the full package. You know it. We know it. Now get out there and stand tall, lead with your heart, and be brave enough to own what you want for yourself. For others to believe in you, you must first believe in yourself. The strengths, passions, and abilities God gave you are not by coincidence; they are your calling. Our challenge for you today is to take inventory of your life: Is there anything at work you need to speak up about? In your home life? Put 2 Timothy 1:7 into practice: approach the conversation with love, knowing that God has not made you timid but with his power you can ask for what you need.

THE SUNSHINE MIND WAY TO . . .
KNOW YOUR OWN WORTH

The first step to asking for what you want is *knowing* what you want. Take a few minutes to write down some of the things on your "want" list:

Now it's time to pray about that list:

Dear God,
I ask you for the strength to [insert from your list]. Please give me the right words to say. Help me to be free from self-doubt and anxiety when I make this request. Thank you that you have equipped me to do all you have called me to do. Amen.

ACCEPT YOURSELF AS WONDERFULLY MADE

I praise you because I am fearfully and
wonderfully made;
your works are wonderful,
I know that full well.

—PSALM 139:14

Tanya

A few years ago I was using the Super Model filter on Instagram. For every post. I mean, hello, it made me look flawless. My pores were gone, my skin glowed, and my face was contoured to perfection. The problem was, I got used to seeing my face through this artificial lens. It got to the point when I saw my unfiltered face in a selfie, I'd think I looked terrible. I went so far as taking side-by-side pictures of myself, one using the Super Model filter and one unfiltered, and sent both pictures to a friend who is a plastic surgeon with a note that said, "What procedures do I need in order to look like this filter?" That is the day I decided to stop using filters on my Instagram. I decided that not only did I not want to portray a fake version of myself to any of my followers, but I also didn't want to brainwash myself into thinking I needed to look like an unattainable, unnatural version of myself.

I am fearfully and wonderfully made" . . . except for the bump on my nose, the bags under my eyes, and oh, that little pooch under my stomach that just will never go away. For many of us, the list can go on and on. But these are things we need to let go of! We are perfectly made by our heavenly Father. Every bump, imperfection, and freckle is ours to own and embrace. Say it with me: "I am fearfully and wonderfully made." When we feel down about ourselves, the best thing to do is to ask God to fill us with his love for us. With that we are able to embrace our truest self, knowing that God created us beautifully in his image and likeness.

THE SUNSHINE MIND WAY TO . . . ACCEPT YOURSELF AS WONDERFULLY MADE

Embrace your face—twenty-four hours filter-free! Join us for twenty-four hours of seeing yourself without a filter on social media. Make sure you hashtag #SunshineMindBook so we can look for your beautiful faces and share them with the world.

OVERCOME IMPOSTER SYNDROME

We are God's masterpiece. He has created us anew in Christ Jesus, so we can do the good things he planned for us long ago.

—EPHESIANS 2:10 NLT

Tanya

Imposter syndrome is a feeling of inadequacy. It is common and impacts a higher percentage of women than men. This chronic self-doubt often is not backed by anything factual. When I'm falling into the imposter syndrome mindset, I ask myself questions of doubt: Who do I think I am? Who am I to be hosting this red-carpet event? Who am I to be auditioning for this show? Who am I to think anyone would want to buy my book? When I find myself asking questions like this, I know my imposter syndrome has taken over and that I need to do something about it. I have to combat self-doubt with affirmations such as these: I am Tanya Rad. I am a modern woman who follows her heart and dreams big. I work my booty off and deserve what I've achieved. Why wouldn't I be on this red carpet? Why wouldn't I audition for this show? Why wouldn't I write this book? So I did, I do, and I will continue to do everything my imposter syndrome makes me question because . . . why not?

The beauty in Ephesians 2:10 is that it reminds us that long ago God prepared our lives and what he wants us to do with them. He has known his plans for your life before you were even born. You don't have to follow someone else's path, and you don't need to follow what society says you should do. You just need to trust in God's plan. If no one is in your corner, you don't have to question or worry, because God is always there cheering you on.

THE SUNSHINE MIND WAY TO . . . OVERCOME IMPOSTER SYNDROME

When you feel imposter syndrome creeping in and you second-guess your ability to do or to be something, pray this prayer and give your emotions to God:

Dear God,
Please watch over me today. See that my words are used for the greater good. May your will be done through the talents and strengths you have blessed me with. Put your hand over me and cover me today so that all my anxieties will flow right out of me and I will be filled with your strength. Thank you for the good things you created me to do. Amen.

PRAY FOR WISDOM

I keep asking that the God of our Lord Jesus Christ, the glorious Father, may give you the Spirit of wisdom and revelation, so that you may know him better.

—EPHESIANS 1:17

Raquelle

When I was in college and thinking about moving from Chicago to LA, someone close to me said, "Raquelle, the grass isn't greener on the other side. It's greener where you water it. I feel like God's telling you to stay here. This is where you're meant to be for your career and your future." Even at eighteen years old, I knew that my own gut feeling was the voice I needed to listen to. I figured if God wanted me to stay in Chicago, God would tell me that too. Thankfully, in this instance I listened to my gut, because if I had listened to what the other person—who was a big voice in my life at the time—told me, I would have missed out on so much that God had planned for me. I don't think God's purpose for us disappears if we choose a different path, so if I'd stayed in Chicago, I wouldn't have necessarily lost my purpose. But it would have looked very different, for sure.

When I moved to LA, it felt tailor-made for me. Everything that has happened to me since I moved here could only have been a plan ordained by God. It was like I was plucked out from a life that I knew and placed directly into a life outside my comfort zone but fully in my purpose. I met my best friends, like-minded people I could experience the world with. I have been able to make positive changes in the world and be a place of support for people close to me. I have always taken this seriously and am forever grateful that God has used me and continues to use me this way.

That thing we call a gut feeling is a blessing given to us by God. It's the wisdom inside each of us that can almost feel like a voice at times, where you just *know* if something is right or wrong. It may sound like an easy thing to discern, but it's not always. Tuning out the strong opinions or feelings of others can be challenging, but at times it's essential to do so. Always tune in to God for his wisdom and revelation. Always listen to your heart, gut, instinct—whatever you want to call it. There you will find God's answer for you and you alone.

THE SUNSHINE MIND WAY TO ... PRAY FOR WISDOM

If you want to make sure that what you're hearing is from God, we recommend praying this prayer (and then listening carefully for God's voice).

Dear God,
I pray that you would give me the wisdom and discernment to know your will today and every day. I pray that you will always open the right doors and close the wrong ones and give me the inner peace and gut feeling to know what you would have me do or say. Thank you for always protecting me. Amen.

BE TRUE TO YOU

Keep a clear conscience before God so that when people throw mud at you, none of it will stick. They'll end up realizing that they're the ones who need a bath.

—1 PETER 3:16-17 MSG

Tanya

Someone I admire professionally once told me that my personality was "too much" for most people. I'd always thought my happy-go-lucky nature was a good thing, so it cut deep to think that all this time, people thought I was annoying. Early on in my podcast, there was a difficult phase when I felt a great amount of pressure to be less like myself. I felt I needed to scale myself back, dim my light, act a little more reserved (and if you know me, you know reserved is *not* my vibe). Despite the pressure to be the quieter, duller version of myself, when push came to shove, I decided to go for it and let my Tanya flag fly. When my cohost Becca and I found out in 2018 that our podcast was nominated for a People's Choice Award for pop podcast of the year, no one was more surprised than I was! To add icing on the cupcake, also nominated was LADYGANG (only my biggest role models), Amy Schumer (my idol), oh, and no big deal—Oprah. Shut up! I almost thought it was a joke, but no, we legit had been nominated alongside some of the biggest names in the industry. I couldn't believe it! This was a God-wink to me right when I most needed it. I am loud. I am silly. I am confused. I am emotional. I am someone who lets it all out, full steam ahead. And that's okay because that's who I am. My personality might have been "too much" for that person, and maybe there are a few others out there who'd agree, but I have a People's Choice Award (spoiler alert: we won . . . two years in a row!) to prove that many people like me just the way I am.

Having a Sunshine Mind means always being true to who you are. Haters gonna hate, always. That's why you have to love yourself extra hard. I (Tanya) was always confident, even as a kid. I was never in the "popular groups," but I always had a lot of friends. I was friends with everyone, was part of every group, and always marched to the beat of my own drum. That inner confidence was a God-given gift, and I still carry that confidence even now. I talk about things that are considered taboo or uncomfortable because I know if I feel a certain way, others probably do too. And that vulnerability is where community is built. I don't shy away from uncomfortable conversations about periods and bleeding and tampons and new products. After all, *why do we hide our tampons up our sleeves when we walk to the bathroom?* I'm not embarrassed or ashamed of my period. And if being my authentic, weird, quirky self gives even one other person the freedom to be themselves, then I am fulfilling God's calling on my life.

THE SUNSHINE MIND WAY TO . . . BE TRUE TO YOU

- Surround yourself with people who love you for you. This gives you freedom to be your true self.
- Check in with yourself and ask, "Why am I doing this? Do I really want this, or is society telling me I want this?"
- What are you passionate about? Often what we are passionate about isn't random; passions can be God's calling in our lives. Dig into those passions; they are your purpose.
- Be comfortable being solo. You never know what you are made of or capable of until you can stand on your own two feet. (If that makes you uncomfortable, start small: go see a movie alone and start from there.)

SERVE OTHERS

Each of you should use whatever gift you have received to serve others, as faithful stewards of God's grace in its various forms.

—1 PETER 4:10

Raquelle

Working in the entertainment industry, I have been around many people who have "everything," yet there is a sense of deep unhappiness. I believe this happens largely because life becomes so self-consumed. It's not even necessarily their fault; it's the nature of the business. Most entertainers enter this field because they love creating music or film. Then they make it big, and life becomes all about self. There are people catering to their every wish, telling them what they want to hear. Yet they can't figure out why they feel so unhappy. In my observation, it is because life has become all about self. When we can get outside of ourselves and find purpose in being of service to others, that's when the real happiness comes. This can happen to anyone in any industry. I use the entertainment industry as an example because I think often the world can look at people who have fame and success and think if I had that I would be happy, but this just isn't true. Happiness comes from service, whatever you choose to do.

The surest way to bring joy to your own life is by serving others. It's easy to dwell on ourselves—what we have, what we want, what we think we're missing. The problem is, this train of thought usually leads to nowhere. Service is a way of life. It's not something you do once a year during the holidays. God gave us gifts and talents to be of service to others. By using your words to help, guide, or uplift people, you are being of service. By using your body to carry, assist, or physically aid, you are being of service. We can serve others as part of our everyday. If I'm (Raquelle here!) having a bad day, I find the strength to serve somebody else, and in return I feel much happier. You're either living your life solely for yourself or living to serve others, as God intended. When we focus on helping other people by sharing our gifts and talents with them, we in turn bless ourselves with the gift of giving.

THE SUNSHINE MIND WAY TO . . . SERVE OTHERS

Always remember to SHINE!

Serving
Him
Ignites
New
Energy

DO A DECLUTTER

God is not a God of disorder but of peace.

—1 CORINTHIANS 14:33

Tanya

I have often found that when I feel anxious or my life feels chaotic, an easy way to clear my mind is to declutter and organize my home. When I see clutter or feel like my closets and drawers are stuffed to the brim, my life feels overwhelming. You know when your closet gets to the point where you can't even slide one more tiny little hanger in there and if you do, something's gonna give? That anxiety bleeds into my personal life. I feel stuffed, suffocated, overwhelmed. We need space in our lives, space for solitude, for time with loved ones, and of course room for fun. We can't function from a space that is filled to the brim. And I need my home to reflect that as well.

One daily practice I do is making my bed every single morning, no matter what. It gives me a sense of accomplishment first thing in the morning. The sun has barely risen, and I've already checked something off my to-do list. This simple act always starts my day off on the right foot.

A clean house leads to a clear mind. If your home is in chaos, that chaotic energy can come through in your daily interactions. But often when you clean your house, you clear your mind. Wherever you can, take a few minutes to tidy up today. Do you have a drawer, a closet, or maybe an entire room that makes you anxious when you look at it? One of those areas that's so overwhelmingly crammed full and unorganized that you don't know where to begin, so you just keep throwing stuff in there? When you shut the drawer or close the door to that closet or room, you can almost imagine it doesn't exist. But you know in the back of your head it's all still there, piling up, collecting dust, and creating chaos in your life. God states in his Word that life does not consist of an abundance of possessions (Luke 12:15). We know from experience that the Sunshine Mind does not thrive in clutter or chaos. It might be able to handle some organized clutter, but cluttered chaos? Nobody needs that!

THE SUNSHINE MIND WAY TO . . . DO A DECLUTTER

Can you dedicate at least thirty minutes today to making a dent in an area of your home that needs decluttering? You don't have to clean an entire room in one go (although major bonus points if you can), but just start somewhere. Donate ten pieces of clothing to a shelter. Toss those expired condiments in your refrigerator. Go through that stack of mail you've let pile up. Clean out your junk drawer. Organize your Monica Geller closet. (For those who don't know that *Friends* reference, google it.) Once you get started, decluttering can be kind of addictive.

Day 10

BE GENEROUS WITH RELATIONSHIPS

A generous person will prosper;
whoever refreshes others will be refreshed.

—PROVERBS 11:25

Raquelle

Even when I haven't had an abundance of finances, I've always had an abundance of relationships, so I make sure I am generous when it comes to connecting people. We all need each other, and in my experience, a little help making personal connections can go a long way. When I think back on my life's journey, I recognize I have achieved so much because others believed in me. My friend Selena is someone who has done this for me. We met over ten years ago now, and I owe much of my career to her generosity in giving me a chance to work on projects alongside her. She validated my work and spoke kindly about me to others, which opened many doors of opportunity for me. If it weren't for her doing this, I wouldn't be where I am now, and I am forever grateful for it. The best thing I can do to show my gratitude is to do the same for others.

God wants you to be generous with whatever you have achieved or been given. There's room for all of us at the top. People often equate generosity with giving money or resources. But generosity is much more than this. You can be generous with your time, love, energy, and space. Think of all the ways you can serve God with those things. It is impossible to serve God without being generous. God showed ultimate generosity by sending his son, Jesus, to die on the cross for our sins. When we look at the life of Jesus, we see that he wasn't wealthy—he was a carpenter—but he was the most generous person who ever lived. He lived generously, showing love and kindness to humanity. Remember, even if you don't have money or material possessions to give, you can always be generous with your relationships.

THE SUNSHINE MIND WAY TO . . . BE GENEROUS WITH RELATIONSHIPS

This book came together as a result of many people being generous with their relationships. Tanya had written a previous book proposal that cost her a lot of time and money. She was crushed when the project ended up on the cutting room floor. She opened up about that experience on her podcast to encourage others who had experienced hearing no in their careers. A listener named Erika heard this story and reached out because her aunt works for a publishing company. Erika wanted to be generous with her relationship in order to help move Tanya forward. This gesture moved everyone to tears.

That same week, Tanya's writer, Allie (whom she had worked with on the previous book proposal), reached out and said she wanted to be generous with her time and do another proposal for Tanya pro bono because she believed in her that much. Tanya then reached out to me, wanting to share this opportunity. One thing led to another and here we are—published authors with a book deal. That all came together through God's grace and people being generous with their relationships.

Think about whether you have relationships and connections you can use to help a friend, family member, or coworker.

LIVE YOUR JOURNEY

I will instruct you and teach you in the way you should go;
I will counsel you with my loving eye on you.

—PSALM 32:8

Tanya

My life journey has been less than conventional in many ways. The way I began my career wasn't the way you were "supposed to" do it. A person doesn't start out in radio by going on the air in Los Angeles. You are "supposed to" start out in a smaller market and get your feet wet and then graduate to a bigger market such as LA. But God had a different path for me. He started me out where he did for his bigger purpose (which I'm still figuring out). Often we choose a certain direction in life because it is the "safest" option. Take this job because of the steady income. Marry this person because you know they come from a good family. Buy this house because you grew up in that neighborhood. We take the path most traveled because we fear the unknown. But God wants us to step outside our fears and live in faith. If you make a bold career move, it may feel risky, but lean into your faith to guide you through. If you want to move across the country for love but you're scared it might not work out, take that leap of faith. Even if that love isn't your one true pairing, maybe God wants you to take that leap because a new career or a life-changing friend awaits you there. "Risks" aren't always risky; sometimes getting out of your comfort zone is where the change happens.

It's perfectly acceptable not to be conventional. Every person's journey is different, and even if people take similar paths, they may not end up at the same destination. We can learn from each other's journeys, but there isn't one right way. Just because one route worked for a friend doesn't guarantee it will garner the same results for you. Let God lead you the right way for you. Your journey is just that—it's *yours*. So listen to the desires of your heart. Focus on what God is calling you toward. It is easy to be swayed by what society says, what you see on your Instagram feed, what your parents tell you they want for your future—the list goes on and on. But today, carve out time to sit and listen to your heart. And then live your own journey.

THE SUNSHINE MIND WAY TO . . . LIVE YOUR JOURNEY

Take some "you time" to ask yourself these questions and reflect on your own personal journey:

- Where do you think God is calling you?
- Which path are you drawn to?
- Where do you feel whole, the best version of yourself?
- What makes your heart happy?
- What are your passions?
- In which situations and places do you feel you are your most authentic and happy self?

Day 12

SHOW LOVE

Do everything in love.

—1 CORINTHIANS 16:14

Tanya

I've always loved the quote, "People tend to forget what you say, but they usually remember how you make them feel." I *tell* my boyfriend all the time that I love him and support his dreams. I *show* him by asking how I can best help and support him. For example, I like to leave him encouraging notes around the house for him to find. These notes consist of meaningful quotes I find and handwrite on little pieces of paper. (Handwritten notes give that extra special personal touch.) I want him to begin each day with a pep in his step, knowing I'm right beside him. I do this daily out of my deep love for him.

Do everything in love." This verse is so simple but also so complex. As we go about our daily lives, we encounter many different people. Most of the time our heads are down, looking at our phones as we wait in line to buy our coffee, board a plane, or hang out in the break room. Today, choose to put your phone down while you go about your day. Instead, focus on the people around you and how you can make a positive impact on another human being, face-to-face. It can be something as simple as smiling at a stranger, buying coffee for the person in line behind you, giving flowers or an encouraging note to a coworker you know is struggling, or striking up a conversation with someone you see every day but have never really talked to. Do everything in love, and then prepare to be amazed by what God can do.

THE SUNSHiNE MiND WAY TO . . . SHOW LOVE

Here are some ideas to show love:

- Cook dinner for someone.
- Drop off a handwritten card in place of sending a text.
- Put together a bouquet of flowers and deliver them yourself.
- Start your partner's or roommate's car in the morning to heat it up (or cool it down).
- Let someone cut ahead of you in line at the grocery store, coffee shop, etc.
- Write an uplifting poem and anonymously leave it in a public place.
- Leave notes on random mirrors, like, "You have a beautiful smile!"
- Drop off a care package for someone who feels under the weather.

Day 13

ACT WiTH BOLDNESS AND CONFIDENCE

Since we have such a hope, we are very bold.

—2 CORiNTHiANS 3:12

Tanya

I am the cheesiest person you know. I was the spirit commissioner at my high school. I give Valentine's Day grams as an adult. I leave sticky notes around the house for my boyfriend to find. Passionate and proud, I've always been this way. And I believe God made me this way for a reason. When applying for full-time jobs in LA, I took the most Tanya Rad approach possible. I designed and sent out baby shoes! Yes, you heard that right—I decorated baby shoes and sent them to every music and media outlet I could find. (That's about twenty-five shoes!) On each shoe I wrote words describing the type of worker I am: driven, passionate, go-getter, positive, persistent, organized. Then I tied my business card around the shoe with a note that said, "Just trying to get my foot in the door." Did I second-guess myself? One thousand percent. Did I worry people would think I was childish or too much or a total weirdo? Yes. But I was honoring the type of person I am, and I hoped the right person would appreciate it.

Fast-forward to Tim Martinez, the promotions director at KIIS FM at the time, getting my shoe and calling me in for an interview, then hiring me on the spot. That was my ticket into working at the very station I had spent my teenage years listening to. I'll never forget how incredible that day felt, and I'll never go against my gut or question why God made me the way he did. Every shoe has a foot, and no two feet are the same.

e bold and confident in who God made you; be your most authentic self. If you feel pressure to act as a different version of yourself to appeal to someone else, ignore it. Recognize the feeling, then come against it, reminding yourself that God created you to be boldly, authentically you.

I (Raquelle here) have always loved the word *bold*. The dictionary describes it as confident and courageous, showing an ability to take risks. I think sometimes people hear the word *bold* and think, "Wow, intense bulldozing type of behavior." But I think boldness is just being clear on something, so much so that you're able to go forth with confidence. When we understand that God created us to be authentically ourselves, we can be clear on what he wants us to do and approach our day-to-day lives boldly.

God gave you the gift of being your own character. Take it and run, honey!

THE SUNSHINE MIND WAY TO . . . ACT WITH BOLDNESS AND CONFIDENCE

What qualities make you, *you*? List them here:

How can you use these qualities to be bold in your actions? For example, are you talented at creating videos? If so, create a visual résumé to send in alongside the traditional one when you apply for a job. Are you a strong leader or task oriented? Ask your desired employer for a fake assignment, and show them how you would accomplish the task if hired. Is there an acquaintance of yours you wish you knew better? Invite them to lunch! If you want something, it is up to you to make it happen.

PROTECT YOUR LIGHT

*Above all else, guard your heart,
for everything you do flows from it.*

—PROVERBS 4:23

Tanya

My coworker Jen taught me this important trick: whenever you're around people who have bad energy, zip yourself inside an imaginary cocoon. Go through the actual motions as if you are zipping something up. Inside is your happy place. Nothing comes in, nothing goes out. When you leave the unpleasant environment, unzip the cocoon and leave it right there. Don't bring it into your car or anywhere else. You leave that contaminated cocoon right where it is. Ever since learning this technique, I've used it when I knew I would be dealing with anyone challenging. I "cocoon up." Try it. You'll be surprised how empowering this action truly is.

We are all bound to encounter people who exude a toxic, upsetting energy. You know the ones: Debbie Downer, Sad Sally, Negative Nancy. As much as you try to wake up with a smile, bounce instead of walk, and be the sunniest, most positive person you can be, you'll inevitably run into one of these individuals. A few minutes spent with this type of person can cast a gloomy storm over what was once a sunshiny day. When you are the light in a room, people will often try to dim your sparkle. Not allowing the ick in others to affect you can seem downright impossible. But it isn't. Simply put, don't allow it! Create an invisible, impermeable shield to protect yourself from taking on somebody else's dark cloud. Guard your heart, and keep your sparkle.

THE SUNSHINE MIND WAY TO . . . PROTECT YOUR LIGHT

DRESS FOR HOW YOU WANT TO FEEL. If you want to keep that pep in your step all day long, wear bright and happy colors that make you feel that way. It works!

ACCESSORIZE IN POSITIVITY. Wear a ring, necklace, or bracelet with a word like *hope* or *joy*, something that brings you back to that feeling when needed.

LEAVE YOURSELF A NOTE. Stick love letters to yourself on things you see often—your steering wheel, the bathroom mirror, the fridge. Use positive messages like, "You're awesome!"

GIVE CHEERFULLY

Each of you should give what you have decided in your heart to give, not reluctantly or under compulsion, for God loves a cheerful giver.

—2 CORINTHIANS 9:7

Tanya

I started out making very little money in the entertainment industry, first working for free as an intern for two years (twelve-hour days between two internships) and then earning minimum wage working part-time. When I achieved a full-time position, I finally received a salary, but I didn't feel worthy of it. It was a big change, and I often wondered what I, a single woman with nobody to care for, was going to do with this upgraded paycheck. But then I realized God had put me in this position to be a blessing. So I chose to bless others. When I am offered services such as hair, nails, makeup, photography, and video editing for free from people in exchange for a photo or tag on social media, as is customary in my industry, I prefer to pay their fee. And I always make sure I give them a shout-out on social media. I love to do this because not only do I see my good fortune as a means to help others, but I also remember when those means of support meant everything to me and helped me get to where I am today.

God wants us to be cheerful givers. We aren't supposed to hold our money tightly. We're supposed to spread it around, to be a blessing to someone else's growing business, to help other entrepreneurs busting their butts to succeed. Want to step it up for New Years? Hire an aspiring makeup artist to take your look to the next level. Enjoying the music of a street performer? Put a few dollars in his jar. The more we empower and lift others up in following their passions and dreams, the more all of us will rise. Decide in your heart what you want to give, and share with others the blessings God has given you.

THE SUNSHINE MIND WAY TO . . . GIVE CHEERFULLY

There are many ways to spread the light and give cheerfully, and not all of them require money!

- Leave positive reviews online.
- Promote a business you love on your social media or by word of mouth.
- Bring awareness to a new business by handing out their business cards or menus to your neighbors.
- Create partnerships by introducing people you know who might want to work together.
- Next time someone gives you great service, ask for their manager and let them know how awesome your experience was because of that employee.
- Write a complimentary note to your server on the receipt (in addition to tipping them kindly, of course).

BE SOMEONE ELSE'S SUNSHINE

Rejoice with those who rejoice, weep with those who weep.

—ROMANS 12:15 ESV

Tanya

I was going through the worst breakup of my life. Sleepless nights, not eating, random crying outbursts at work. Everyone knew I was a mess, and it was obvious I was broken. One day my coworker Patty showed up at the office with a necklace for me. It was a simple silver necklace with the word *hope* inscribed on it. Up until this point, Patty and I had hardly exchanged pleasantries. We weren't very warm to each other, as we hadn't exactly gotten off on the right foot. "What's this?" I asked Patty as she gave me the necklace. "This belongs to you now," she replied. She too had experienced a painful breakup in her past. She said my experience reminded her a lot of what she had gone through when her heart had been shattered. Someone gave her this necklace and told her to hold on and never give up hope.

Her beautiful, thoughtful gesture brought me to tears. I was touched by how this necklace had served its purpose in Patty's life and now she wanted to give it to me, even though we weren't close friends. We finally "saw" each other that day. We shared stories. We exchanged words of encouragement. We became each other's biggest cheerleaders, personally and professionally. I believe God put Patty in my life for a special reason, and the way our friendship developed taught me a lesson I've kept in mind ever since: be someone else's sunshine whenever you can.

A simple gesture can leave a lasting impact on another person's life. Being the light in someone's darkest moment is one of the most important actions we can take. When someone is going through a dark time, people often don't know what to do, so they do nothing. Not because they don't want to but because it may feel too vulnerable or they don't want to overstep their bounds. The truth is, everybody wants to feel loved and noticed. Empathy is one of the most beautiful things we can extend to another person. Empathy says *I'm with you*. When someone is going through heartbreak or divorce—*I'm with you*. When someone has lost a loved one—*I'm with you*. When someone has lost a job—*I'm with you*. When someone got the promotion of their dreams—*I'm with you*. When someone reached a goal they never imagined—*I'm with you*. Showing empathy meets someone right where they are, and that is what God calls us to do.

THE SUNSHINE MIND WAY TO . . . BE SOMEONE ELSE'S SUNSHINE

You can be the sun shining through on someone's cloudy day.

- Order them delivery from their favorite restaurant.
- Invite them to go for a walk.
- Write them a letter of encouragement.
- Do their chores for them—take out their garbage, walk their dogs, collect their mail.
- Go for a drive together and stop for a treat.
- Watch a funny movie with them and serve their favorite snacks.
- Put together a gift basket of their favorite things.

GIVE IT YOUR ALL
AND CRUSH IT

A sluggard's appetite is never filled,
but the desires of the diligent are fully satisfied.

—PROVERBS 13:4

Raquelle

I remember in high school, like many other girls, my social life was a huge priority. There were times—okay, many times—when I would do the bare minimum just to complete an assignment. After I turned it in, I would never feel great because I knew I could have done better. Then in the instances when I really *did* take my time and complete my homework to the best of my ability, I would feel so great (and of course get a better grade!). This lesson has continued beyond my studies, of course. As an adult, I know that a lazy workout or a half-done job might check something off the list, but it doesn't bring full satisfaction because we're meant to live life to our fullest potential and give it our all.

Always know that when you do your best and give something your all, it's not just enough—it's more than enough. It's when we *don't* work to our potential that we feel empty or unsatisfied. If we give a lazy performance, simply going through the motions to get something done, we won't feel accomplished or proud of ourselves. It's only when we crush a project and perform to the best of our abilities that we fulfill our potential and shine from within. Be diligent about the work you have to do. Give it your all—and crush it!

THE SUNSHiNE MiND WAY TO . . .
GiVE IT YOUR ALL AND CRUSH IT

Pause for a moment to take inventory of the different areas of your life. Close your eyes and breathe in deeply. Are there any areas where you know you are aren't giving your all? Maybe it's at work, or something as simple as making your bed. Maybe it's being on your phone at dinner instead of engaging in conversation with the other people at the table. Whatever it is, take mental note and think about how you can show up fully for yourself or for others this week. What does that look like for you?

BE AN ENCOURAGING FRIEND

Encourage one another and build each other up, just as in fact you are doing.

—1 THESSALONIANS 5:11

Tanya

My friends and I have been through many seasons together. Heartbreak. (And let me tell ya, I'm the go-to girlfriend for breakups. Wine night? Cry-over-a-sad-movie night? Flower deliveries? Good-morning texts? I'm your girl!) Loss. Career successes and career failures. Family turbulence.

Each season requires a different type of time and commitment from me as a friend. I've learned that sometimes you have to stretch yourself a little thin to be there for someone who is going through a hard time—and that's okay. At the end of the day, you can't be a perfect friend. You will mess up. You will let someone down. You won't be there in the way someone needs you to be. But let your friends know you love them, and they will always know your heart is in the right place.

Our lives are built on relationships—friendships, romances, coworker bonds, family connections, and most importantly, our relationships with ourselves and with God. But we often take our deepest friendships for granted. These kinds of friendships require work, often just as much as romantic relationships do. They require intention, sacrifice, compromise, time, and attention. You may be in a different season of life than some of your friends, and that's only natural. Just remember that being open and communicating is the key to friendship longevity. If you've messed up in a friendship and maybe you've both let your egos get in the way, today is the day to reach out. Focus on encouraging your friend. Build her up. And be there for her in the best way you can.

THE SUNSHINE MIND WAY TO . . .
BE AN ENCOURAGING FRIEND

What are the people in your life going through? Think of some ways you can encourage them and build them up, like sending an uplifting note or showing up with supplies for an at-home spa day (face masks, nail polish) or movie night (popcorn, ice cream). Sometimes people just need someone to be there, going through the motions with them so they don't feel so alone. However you decide to share the light, post a video or a picture with the hashtag #SunshineMindBook so we can continue to spread the light with you!

FiND FAMiLY IN FRIENDSHIPS

The LORD himself goes before you and will be with you; he will never leave you nor forsake you. Do not be afraid; do not be discouraged.

—DEUTERONOMY 31:8

Raquelle

I was recently talking to a friend who has experienced a lot of turmoil in her home life. Despite this, she has handled everything well. I asked her to share with me what she felt has been helpful. She said the first thing we are tempted to do when we experience family tension is to hide it because we often feel vulnerable or embarrassed about it. But when we confide in a trusted friend, we realize everyone is going through something, and we immediately feel less alone. She also said that when she was younger, she would share with too many people, which leads to too many different ideas and too many opinions. (Also, not everyone is looking out for you.) When it comes to your closest confidants, choose quality over quantity. It's not about how many you have, it's about who will look out for your best interests.

amily tension can be extremely unsettling. When there is tension and times are tough, we can feel isolated and alone. But the Bible tells us the Lord will never leave us (Hebrews 13:5) and we don't need to feel afraid. When there is tension and times are tough, we can feel isolated and alone. But the Bible tells us in the book of Joshua 1:5, "As I was with Moses, so I will be with you; I will never leave you nor forsake you." What a comfort to know that amid a family fight or tension in the home, we can still experience the peace of God. It's also a good idea to find a community you can talk through stuff with. If you don't already have this community, pray that you will find people who will let you vent and who you can talk to openly while still keeping your family issues confidential. We all need people in our lives who offer us a safe place for sharing and who give us unconditional empathy and support. Proverbs 18:24 says, "There is a friend who sticks closer than a brother." Know that even if your family situation is a mess, you can always find family in your friends.

THE SUNSHINE MIND WAY TO . . . FIND FAMILY IN FRIENDSHIPS

Think about your closest friendships. Are these people like family to you? Have they been there for you in your hardest moments? How can you be there for them? Then think of your family. Pray this prayer and ask God to heal any broken family relationships you might have.

Dear God,
Thank you that you have placed me in this family for a reason. Please comfort me during this time of tension. I pray that you would give me the right person or people to open up to and that you would give me peace that surpasses understanding. Amen.

CHANGE YOUR MINDSET

Do not conform to the pattern of this world, but be transformed by the renewing of your mind. Then you will be able to test and approve what God's will is—his good, pleasing and perfect will.

Raquelle

The way I renew my mind, like Romans 12:2 says, is through spending time with God—going for prayer and worship drives in my car, taking long walks, choosing to pray about disappointments and discouragement instead of getting even or becoming angry. When I do these things, I truly experience God's love and peace every single time. All the other negative stuff goes away. The Bible says, "In your anger do not sin" (Ephesians 4:26). When someone hurts me, it's okay for me to feel angry, but it's not okay to retaliate. I need to remember not to conform to the world's way of reacting but instead choose to take the high road. My responsibility is to acknowledge my anger but to respond with maturity.

R omans 12:2 is one of our favorite Bible verses because the second we conform to the things of this world, we get caught up in harmful habits: comparing ourselves to others, not feeling good about ourselves, giving in to temptations. But when we are transformed by the renewing of our minds (a.k.a., spending time with God), we can discern what God's will is, and this enables us to make wise choices. We love The Message version of this passage: "Don't become so well-adjusted to your culture that you fit into it without even thinking. Instead, fix your attention on God. You'll be changed from the inside out. Readily recognize what he wants from you, and quickly respond to it. Unlike the culture around you, always dragging you down to its level of immaturity, God brings the best out of you, develops well-formed maturity in you." When we are mature with wisdom and live out God's best for us, we don't necessarily live lives free of challenges, because no one's life is perfect. But we *can* live lives filled with peace of mind, which comes from God, and discernment about the right choices to make.

THE SUNSHINE MIND WAY TO . . . CHANGE YOUR MINDSET

When you're tempted to respond to a person or a situation with anger, take a moment to change your mindset.

- Don't respond right away. Take time to process your feelings and articulate your thoughts.
- Remember that it's okay to cry.
- Be accountable for your actions.
- Pray about the situation and surrender it to God.

CELEBRATE OTHERS

If you harbor bitter envy and selfish ambition in your hearts, do not boast about it or deny the truth. Such "wisdom" does not come down from heaven but is earthly, unspiritual, demonic. For where you have envy and selfish ambition, there you will find disorder and every evil practice.

—JAMES 3:14–16

Tanya

My friend Becca had recently finished filming *The Bachelor* and was starting to navigate her path in the entertainment industry. Becca had received an amazing career opportunity filling in for our local news entertainment anchor for the entire morning shift. This assignment was my dream job. I live and breathe pop culture, and at that time I had never done TV, so in my eyes this was the gig of all gigs. I could have easily been consumed with jealously, but instead I was overwhelmed with happiness for Becca. Even though this opportunity was something I had always wanted, I knew my time would come. This was her moment. I brought her cupcakes that said "good luck" and let her know I was praying for her to crush it. I'll admit it's a lot easier to act this way when it's happening to a good friend versus a stranger, but I try to invoke that celebratory spirit no matter who I'm celebrating.

God doesn't want us to be consumed with jealousy, bitterness, or selfishness. Yet society has made us believe we are in constant competition with one another. But not every opportunity is meant for you, and ultimately God closes doors that aren't yours and opens ones that are. It's not about understanding when or why but trusting in his perfect plan for you. Jealousy and bitterness are ugly. They can cause you to do ugly things, like saying hurtful words or spreading gossip, and this is not who God created you to be. If we let jealousy overtake us, we can end up doing and saying things we will regret. But you'll never regret taking the high road and celebrating others.

THE SUNSHINE MIND WAY TO . . . CELEBRATE OTHERS

My best friend Becca and I are opposite in our love languages, but we both work hard to speak to each other in the way that makes the other feel loved. I love FaceTime; Becca hates it. I prefer to sit on the same side of the table while we eat; Becca prefers sitting across. I like wearing T-shirts with each other's faces on them; Becca, not so much. But we give love the way the other likes to receive it. Here are some ideas for celebrating others:

A BIG CAREER OPPORTUNITY. Buy them cupcakes that say "Good Luck!"

BIRTHDAY CELEBRATIONS. Get a balloon for every year of their life, and write on each balloon one reason you love them.

HEARTBREAK. Make a basket filled with their favorite things (a bottle of wine, a breakup book, their favorite treats, etc.).

FEELING DOWN. Help them clean or organize their place to give them some pep in their step.

JUST BECAUSE. Order shirts with each other's faces on them and have a girls' night out.

PREPARE FOR PERFECT LOVE

There is no fear in love. But perfect love drives out fear, because fear has to do with punishment. The one who fears is not made perfect in love.

Tanya

For many years I closed myself off to love because I did not want to crawl back into that dark shell it had taken me so long to get out of after experiencing a rough breakup. I know this fear plagues many of us when it comes to romantic love. The fear of disappointment. The fear of it not working out. The fear of rejection. Matters of the heart are tricky and difficult. But we can't operate from a place of fear—in any area of our lives.

How did I eventually overcome this fear? I knew God had put the desire for marriage in my heart. He had planted this desire for lifelong partnership, family, and teamwork so deep in my heart that I *knew* he had plans to fulfill it. So with faith in my heart I began dating again. Don't get me wrong—a lot of my dating life led to disappointment, more heartbreak, and tears. But I was getting closer and closer to where I was meant to be. And to me, that was everything. If you are in a season of pain or healing from a broken heart, I want to encourage you not to let heartbreak get in the way of your destiny. Be fearless. Be faith-filled. This is the way God intended us to live in his perfect love.

F ear is the opposite of faith. God did not create us to live in fear but in faith and trust in him. So why are we constantly bogged down by fear in many areas of our lives? And specifically, in romantic relationships? Heartbreak is a feeling we've all experienced (and if you haven't, bless your heart and all its glory). It's a feeling of complete and utter helplessness. A feeling like your heart has shattered into a million pieces while you struggle to see how it will ever mend. The sleepless nights. The cry sessions. The fear you will never find happiness again. When love knocks you down, why would you want to get back in the ring again? Why would you want to let someone in, only to experience that same pain when it doesn't work out again? Faith is the answer. Faith and trusting in God's perfect love and timing. Remember, there is no fear in love.

THE SUNSHINE MIND WAY TO . . . PREPARE FOR PERFECT LOVE

Write down all your fears about relationships. Every single negative thought or fear or doubt that enters your head—write it down on a piece of paper. Once every thought is out of your head and on that piece of paper, *rip it to shreds, baby!* (Or you can pull a Tanya and burn that paper to ashes, but I don't want to promote pyro here. This is a happy, sunshine-filled space!)

Day 23

FORGIVE YOURSELF

*Whoever conceals their sins does not prosper,
but the one who confesses and renounces them
finds mercy.*

—PROVERBS 28:13

Raquelle

We all make mistakes. We let people down. We don't always live up to our standards of the kind of family member and friend we want to be. So when I think of Proverbs 28:13 and consider the things I have had to forgive myself for, the easiest way I have been able to do this is by immediately owning what I have done. I make it a point not to fall into pride by justifying my mistake but completely owning and acknowledging it to the other person, if someone else was involved. Doing this leaves no room for shame or time for self-deprecating thoughts, just grace, which is what we all need. Whatever the situation is, even if it doesn't involve another person, it's so important that we not only forgive ourselves but that we understand God forgives us too. It is because of this that we get to live free and choose better going forward.

roverbs 28:13 is an important verse because we have found, in many conversations with friends over the years, that one of the biggest things holding people back is not being able to forgive themselves. If God forgives us, why is it so hard to forgive ourselves? When we make mistakes like cheating on a test or breaking a promise, we can fall into a place of shame and guilt. Of course we have to acknowledge what we did and face the consequences of our actions, but we also need to forgive ourselves. God forgives us, so why should we hold on to our mistakes? We can talk about them with a trusted friend if we need to, but ultimately we must bring them to God. If we always held on to our past and spent our time dwelling on all the bad decisions we've made, we would all live in turmoil all the time. The truth is, we are constantly growing and evolving, and with that growth comes learning from our mistakes and accepting God's forgiveness. And if God forgives us and accepts us, we should forgive ourselves and live free!

THE SUNSHINE MIND WAY TO . . . FORGIVE YOURSELF

If you have trouble forgiving yourself and letting go of your mistakes, speak this affirmation to yourself:

I am human.
I make mistakes.
I learn from those mistakes.
I will do better.
I love myself.
God forgives me.
I forgive myself.

BELIEVE IN YOUR PURPOSE

I can do all things through Christ who strengthens me.

Raquelle

The dictionary defines *purpose* as "the reason for which something is done or created or for which something exists." Purpose can be easy to think about when we think of objects or an event. We know why and how each thing exists and serves its purpose, but when it comes to ourselves it becomes much more complex. Why am I here? Am I walking in my purpose? These questions we ask ourselves throughout life. We can wonder, "Am I here to become CEO of my dream company? Start a family? Invent the next big tech thing?" The list goes on. But when we are talking about a God-purpose, everything changes. I define our God-given purpose as knowing and loving God intimately and deeply and in return loving others, then using the desires in your heart and things that move you to compassion to work hard and honor God with whatever it is you choose to do.

Sometimes we get overwhelmed with big dreams for fulfilling our purpose, but it's important to remember what the Bible says, that we can do all things through Christ who strengthens us (Philippians 4:13). For me, I know I am in my purpose when I feel peace. Sometimes I can even be dealing with a chaotic circumstance, but if it's in my purpose, whether that be working on a project or being there for a friend, there's a peace that exists when it's something I am meant to be working on or being there for someone close to me. It's also important to note that in my early twenties I worked jobs that I didn't necessarily feel were my purpose, like being an assistant (I'm not administrative savvy at all). But I needed a job, and it led me to my next job that was in my purpose. But still there is a peace that comes in knowing you are getting a paycheck and working toward your dreams. Living out your purpose is a lifelong journey that is constantly evolving, and everyone's purpose is unique to them. So always remember that Christ has strengthened you to live out a purpose unique to his divine plan for your life.

To do anything well, you have to believe in your God-given potential and purpose. If you doubt yourself, see yourself as less than, compare yourself to other people, or think you're not good enough, you will never completely fulfill your purpose. We are all capable of doing what God has called us to do, but if you don't believe in yourself, you'll never be able to fully step into your purpose the way that God designed for you. It is important that we believe we can do all things through Christ because the more we believe, the more we have the confidence to fully step into our God-given purpose and potential without being swayed by our own negative thoughts or the opinions of others.

THE SUNSHINE MIND WAY TO . . .
BELIEVE IN YOUR PURPOSE

We've always believed that our passions are not random. Rather, they are our God-given purpose. Don't ignore these passions in your life. They are your calling. Identifying these can be tricky, but the more you experience life, the more apparent they become.

Every year, Tanya makes vision boards for goals she wants to accomplish. She checks in on those at the beginning of each month. Tip: When you pay your rent check on the first of every month, use that as a marker to check in on your life goals as well.

A few books we recommend:

The Hollywood Commandments by DeVon Franklin
What I Know For Sure by Oprah Winfrey
I've Been Thinking . . . by Maria Shriver

Podcasts we love:

On Purpose with Jay Shetty
Oprah's Super Soul Conversations

We also suggest checking in with your pastor or campus pastors on where they see your strengths and how you can minister in your daily life.

Day 25

LIVE OUT YOUR FAITH

Set your hearts on things above.

—COLOSSIANS 3:1

Tanya

The story of how this devotional came to be was very much in God's hands. Many years before we felt it on our hearts to write this book, I wrote a book proposal that was all about dating. I have a weekly podcast where I tell all my dating stories, many of which sound like they are straight out of a movie. I spent seven years in the LA dating scene, which honestly felt more like one hundred years. Every type of guy you can imagine—I dated him. The dating book I planned to write was light-hearted, fun, and something I felt passionate about. But I didn't follow my gut on a couple of big decisions. I didn't go with what God had put on my heart. I let myself be swayed. Needless to say, that dating book was left on the cutting room floor. No one wanted it.

At the time, that felt like the ultimate rejection. But rejection is sometimes God's redirection. See, what I wanted to do with my book (and with my life) was to encourage people to hope and dream. To let them know it was okay to be authentically themselves and not to settle when it came to asking for the desires of their hearts.

In 2020 my cohost and I did a yearly wrap-up on the podcast and discussed our peaks and valleys of that year. I talked about my failed book proposal—the hours lost, the money wasted, the rejection that followed. But God had bigger plans for me. He put it on my heart to write a devotional that encouraged others to never give up. My cowriter Allie, who worked with me on my failed book proposal, reached out to me, saying she would work with me pro bono on this proposal because she believed in me that much. Raquelle had also reached out to me about wanting to help people who were feeling lost and helpless after this tragic pandemic. And finally, a *Scrubbing In* listener reached out and told me her aunt worked in publishing and wanted to meet with me. This was the book I was meant to write! God put all the pieces of the puzzle together. I've never felt more purpose-filled about anything in my career. This wasn't just magic, this was God's will.

God's plans are to prosper us and to have us do important work for him. When something doesn't work out, don't be discouraged. That's all part of his plan. When we experience failure or rejection, God tells us, "It's okay. Keep trusting me, I have a plan for you."

A friend of mine (this is Tanya btw) from church would tell me my job was a form of ministry. I know, how can a girl who talks on the radio for a living be a way, shape, or form of ministry? But I quickly realized that spreading the good news of Jesus and his love is a form of ministry, and that was something I enjoyed doing. This devotional was what I was meant to create. A dating book is fun for a laugh, but this project had the heart behind it that was meant to be.

THE SUNSHINE MIND WAY TO . . . LIVE OUT YOUR FAITH

It's a common misconception that everything we want to achieve has to be done early on, in our twenties and by midthirties. Whenever Raquelle and I become anxious about our goals not being met as quickly as we'd like, we review this list of incredibly successful people who didn't hit their professional stride until later in life. They held on to their hearts' desires, and God had big plans for them.

Vera Wang broke into fashion at forty.

Julia Child published her first book at fifty.

Morgan Freeman got his big break in Hollywood acting at fifty.

Ken Jeong was a doctor and didn't become an actor until he was thirty-eight.

Viola Davis got her first big break and Oscar nomination at forty-three.

Bethenny Frankel was $20,000 in debt when she sold part of her company for $100 million in her late thirties.

Martha Stewart was a stockbroker until publishing her first cookbook at forty-one.

Samuel L. Jackson, after decades of small roles, finally got his big break at forty-six.

PUT OFF YOUR OLD SELF AND BE MADE NEW

You were taught, with regard to your former way of life, to put off your old self, which is being corrupted by its deceitful desires; to be made new in the attitude of your minds; and to put on the new self, created to be like God in true righteousness and holiness.

−EPHESIANS 4:22−24

Raquelle

Sometimes I think about my own life and how it relates to these verses from Ephesians. I grew up in the church and always believed in God, but I didn't experience the fullness of the new self until I started putting my faith into practice in my late teens and then fully putting it into practice in my midtwenties. Today, having a relationship with God is so much a part of my everyday life that everything I do—whether it's decisions I make, the way I speak to my friends, or how I interact with strangers—flows out of the new self, which is a life with Christ at the center. When I wasn't living this way, I would make decisions that didn't align with the person I wanted to be and the life I wanted to have. I'm not perfect, but I'm grateful that because I have put off my old self and the mindset that was, I am able to live as a new self, fully surrendered to God. I can now live a life overflowing with abundance and purpose.

Wow, these verses can feel like a lot of pressure. Put off my old self? Put on my new self? What does that even mean? Ephesians 4:22–24 is talking about a life *before* and a life *after* Christ. To break it down, here's what the verse is saying: Before we knew what it was like to be in relationship with God, some things troubled us and tempted us. After we come to Christ, these don't necessarily go away, but our mindset about them changes. Once we are filled with God's love, righteousness, and holiness, we have help in combating the challenges that come our way. Putting on the new self gives us a chance to live with peace in spite of our circumstances and a trust in something greater than ourselves.

THE SUNSHINE MIND WAY TO . . . PUT OFF YOUR OLD SELF AND BE MADE NEW

Every day is a new day, a chance to start fresh. Yesterday is in the past. Whether your struggle is serious and big or seemingly small, it's never too late to make it right.

Daily we face forks in the road. We have to decide whether to partake in certain conversations, to spend time with certain friend groups, to react to negative behavior in one way or the other, to spend our time productively or to check out. When at a crossroads, think about your relationship with God. Which direction (choice) would be done with love, in service of others, and have a positive ripple effect on your life and the lives of others? Avoid the path the old self would have taken, and choose the path of righteousness and holiness.

FIND YOUR PATH

Trust in the Lord with all your heart
and lean not on your own understanding;
in all your ways submit to him,
and he will make your paths straight.

—PROVERBS 3:5-6

Raquelle

I think it's awesome that some people have always known what they wanted to do or be. They likely took a path where there's a set plan to getting where they needed to go, like becoming a teacher, doctor, or lawyer. They went to school, checked off the required courses, got the degree, and entered the field they worked so hard to get into. That is amazing! But many of you, just like me, probably didn't know which path to take. In college I thought I wanted to be a journalist. I didn't end up going the traditional route of getting a broadcast journalism degree, then working my way up into a top market. Instead, I hopped around doing different jobs, and now I host an interview series on my podcast. One thing always leads to the next, and while my path may have been less defined than some, it still led to what I am doing today. I believe God has set forth all of our paths with intention, whether they are straight or swervy.

Sometimes you have to find out what's not for you in order to figure out what *is*. This applies to pretty much everything: dating, jobs, cars, hobbies, fashion, home décor—seriously, all of it! A friend of ours thought she wanted a boyfriend who loved going out. But then she dated someone who wanted to go out and party all the time and realized maybe she wants more of a homebody who'd rather spend quality time together. Now she's another step closer to finding the right partner because she knows what she doesn't want. Try not to worry about the past and what didn't work out, though. Just focus on taking the next right step, and it will lead you to where you are meant to be. When you put your trust in the Lord, there is no wrong move. Be bold and have faith in your God-given discernment, and God will make sure you're headed toward the best plan for your life.

THE SUNSHINE MIND WAY TO . . . FIND YOUR PATH

Whenever you experience what seems like a setback, acknowledge what went "wrong." Then recognize what went right. Below are some "Yes, but" ideas to get you started:

Yes, I lost _____, but I gained _____.

Yes, I failed at _____, but I now know _____.

Yes, I missed _____, but next time I can _____.

Yes, I didn't _____, but God has a better plan for me and always has my best interests in mind.

REFRESH YOUR SOUL

The LORD is my shepherd, I lack nothing.
He makes me lie down in green pastures,
he leads me beside quiet waters,
he refreshes my soul.

−PSALM 23:1-3

Raquelle

Throughout my life, I've had to change schools, houses, and friends several times. I moved from Chicago to England, back to Chicago, then to LA. All of this required adapting to new surroundings and putting myself out there to make new friends, which isn't easy when people have spent years together and already have established friend groups. So I continually had to go into situations asking God to give me the confidence to be myself and trusting that he was putting the right people in my path. Adjusting to new surroundings requires a lot of energy, but I found that wherever I was, the presence of God would refresh me and help me to be confident. Even now, whenever I face a tough time, I have found Psalm 23 to be my anchor, teaching me that no matter where I go or what I face, the Lord will refresh my soul. I truly lack nothing.

In tougher moments, God's presence was the only thing that didn't change. When I didn't have friends, God was there. He was my rock. My faith allowed me to go confidently into new situations where I had nobody, to be strong in creating a new life for myself, because I knew I wasn't alone. God was there all along, and he knows me better than anyone else ever will—the ultimate friend and refresher of my soul.

Reading Psalm 23:1–3 now, despite having read it many other times, still gives me (still Raquelle here) the chills. A shepherd is someone who tends, feeds, and guards the flock. Think about that. The God who created heaven and earth tends to and guards each and every one of us. We lack nothing. He will satisfy our every need. Think about something you're worried about. Then visualize green pastures, quiet waters. This calming visual represents how God refreshes our souls.

THE SUNSHINE MIND WAY TO . . . REFRESH YOUR SOUL

If you feel especially worried or stressed about a situation in your life, read Psalm 23:1–3 and then pray this prayer:

Dear God,
Thank you that you are my shepherd. Today I surrender [thing that is causing you worry and stress]. I pray that you would refresh my soul. Amen.

IMPROVE YOURSELF

An intelligent heart acquires knowledge,
and the ear of the wise seeks knowledge.

—PROVERBS 18:15 ESV

Raquelle

To grow and become the best version of yourself, you have to be always learning. If you're not learning, you're not evolving, because there's always more to learn. I remember listening to an interview that Oprah did with Dr. Maya Angelou. Oprah asked Maya, who was in her seventies at the time, if she considered herself wise. Maya had replied, "Well, I'm en route. I'm certainly on the road."[1] Interesting how a woman who is known for being among the wisest in the world would consider herself still learning and evolving even in her later years. I think her words are true and profound because we never fully arrive. We must stay committed to seeking knowledge and improving ourselves.

I (Raquelle again!) have always valued the wisdom of people beyond my years, who have lived more life than me. I remember as a kid always wanting to be at the adult table so I could hear what they had to say and as a teenager watching YouTube videos of commencement speeches and leaders, learning from their wisdom. To this day some of my most favorite conversations are with my grandparents and people much older than me. People further along in life than us have knowledge and wisdom they can share with us. And Proverbs 18:15 reminds us how important it is to seek knowledge to improve ourselves.

One thing I, Tanya, have had to learn in my thirties that I wish I would have known earlier is the importance of setting boundaries. As a control freak, I wanted to control every aspect of my life, but trying to control others created a lot of turmoil and unnecessary stress for me. Once I learned how to set boundaries and control my expectations, my life shifted in a lighter, brighter direction.

Here are a few books that helped me in this area:

Boundaries by Dr. Henry Cloud and Dr. John Townsend
Codependent No More by Melody Beattie
Untamed by Glennon Doyle

Three ways to gain knowledge this week:

1. Have a conversation with someone who is spiritually wise, whether it be a grandparent, a boss, a mentor. Ask them to tell you some of their most important life lessons.
2. Watch a commencement speech. They are filled with people sharing their greatest life lessons.
3. Pray about something that's bothering you. Ask God to give you wisdom on what to do about it. I have found that when I pray about upsetting situations, God gives me revelation and guidance.

GET GUIDANCE

If you don't know what you're doing, pray to the Father. He loves to help. You'll get his help, and won't be condescended to when you ask for it. Ask boldly, believingly, without a second thought.

—JAMES 1:5-8 MSG

Raquelle

I have always been a yes-person, which can be great but can also cause me to spread myself too thin. I've found that in asking myself which opportunities to take and which ones to say no to, it's important to figure out my mission and purpose. If you don't know exactly what your mission and purpose are, think about your core values and passions. What moves you? What fires you up? What catches—and keeps—your interest? Answering these questions can help you figure out your purpose. For me, my focus is working on projects that advance the good that others do and spread a message of hope and love. Taking on opportunities that align with my purpose is important. When I'm deciding what to say yes to, I also rely on my God-given discernment and pray and listen for the answer.

ake a moment to be still and pray. Whatever it is in your life that you've been questioning, bring it to God so he can show you whether something is a yes or a no. James 1:8 says to ask boldly. To me, that means knowing and understanding that God is a loving Father and that we never need to give a second thought to him wanting to help us. When we come to God in prayer, asking for what we need, we can ask confidently, knowing that he loves us, hears us, and wants the best for us.

THE SUNSHINE MIND WAY TO . . . GET GUIDANCE

When you're uncertain about the next step to take or when you have a big decision to make, pray this prayer and then listen closely for God's voice:

Dear God,
I need your guiding light in my life right now. Help me to know your will. I am unsure of my next step forward, but I ask you to be my shield and my rock. I pray that your strong conviction will come over me and move me in the direction I'm meant to go. Amen.

PRIORITIZE REST

By the seventh day God had finished the work he had been doing; so on the seventh day he rested from all his work. Then God blessed the seventh day and made it holy, because on it he rested from all the work of creating that he had done.

—GENESIS 2:2-3

Raquelle

We live in a world where people think if you're the busiest, you've made it. We have a sleep-is-for-the-weak mentality. I remember reading a story about Arianna Huffington, founder of the *Huffington Post*. She was working so hard and getting so little sleep that one day, she collapsed at her desk and woke up in a pool of blood. Her diagnosis was exhaustion. She is someone who the world looks at as a leader, someone who has achieved incredible things in her life, but none of that meant anything if she couldn't get adequate sleep, making her able to function. This is a great lesson for all of us, but especially for young people trying to figure out their careers and climb the ladder of success, no matter the cost. Without adequate rest, we can't function.

God designed rest as a necessary and important part of life. The earlier we learn this, the less likely we will be to burn out or have a breakdown. It's easy to let FOMO (fear of missing out) get the better of us and feel frustrated if we can't stay up as late as our friends. Sometimes we know we need rest, but instead we go out after a long day of work, trying to justify getting only a few hours of sleep. But many of us need a full eight hours to function at our best. This means we can't do everything—and that's okay. It's better to be the best version of yourself at the select social activities you do show up at instead of spreading yourself too thin and not being able to do anything well. The fact that God designed an entire *day* just for rest is a great reminder that rest is not negotiable; we can't live without it. This week, challenge yourself to get a healthy amount of sleep each night, and see how it changes your day-to-day activities—the amount of work you get done, how you interact with others, the way you feel physically and emotionally. God designed you to take time to rest, so prioritize that need he created in you.

THE SUNSHINE MIND WAY TO . . . PRIORITIZE REST

Here's our favorite Sunshine Mind sleep routine:

- Schedule rest like you would an appointment. Take at least fifteen to thirty minutes a day to do whatever relaxes you.
- Instead of scrolling on your phone, sip chamomile tea and read a book or write in a journal.
- Dab a touch of sleep-inducing lavender essential oil behind your ears.
- If you live in a noisy area, invest in a white noise machine and turn it on at bedtime.
- Go to sleep in total darkness.

Sweet dreams!

Day 32

WALK IN INTEGRITY

The Lord gives wisdom;
  from his mouth come knowledge and
    understanding;
he stores up sound wisdom for the upright;
  he is a shield to those who walk in integrity,
guarding the paths of justice
  and watching over the way of his saints.

—PROVERBS 2:6–8 ESV

Tanya

I need to share a story about a man I call Mr. Wilshire. I met him when we were both stuck in LA traffic one day. He rolled down his window and asked me for my number, then called me on the spot to ask me out. This was when I was in my "say yes to everything and be open" phase of dating, so I took this as a sign and ran with it. I had a feeling this guy was no good, but I pushed that feeling aside and kept going on dates with him because, well, that's what hopeful hearts do. Plus, I was invested in this guy and felt giddy about him. We made dinner plans one Saturday night. That day was the Veuve Clicquot polo match, an event in LA where people dress up and drink champagne all day while pretending to watch polo. It's supercute and totally my vibe. I went with my best friend Becca, and after our morning of drinking champs, we decided to grab lunch near the polo fields.

Now, let me describe LA to you—when you are on the Westside, you don't leave the Westside. When you live in the heart of LA, you don't cross over that freeway. Because, traffic. So Becca and I were deep in the Westside, waiting for a lunch table, when Mr. Wilshire himself came strolling down the street, hand in hand and lip on lip with a beautiful brunette.

66

Mr. Wilshire lived in the heart of the city, but he was on the Westside, clearly so as not to be seen. If this man I was supposed to be going on a date with *in a matter of hours* was double-booking on that day, I didn't even want to know how many other women he was dating at the same time. God was watching over me in that situation. He had given me the gut feeling that this guy was no good, but I'd ignored him. So he went and put it right in front of my face. Also, I owe Becca a special shout-out for fully taking over that awkward run-in. She introduced herself and made small talk while my jaw was on the floor. And for anyone wondering, I stood him up for our date that night.

God is a shield to those who walk in integrity. If you are living an upright life, God knows your heart and will be your shield, even when you don't see his work behind the scenes. If you are traveling down a destructive path, God will interrupt you and steer you toward a different—and better—one. If you are with the wrong person or are about to make a wrong decision, you better believe he will find a way to steer you in the right direction. If you choose to walk in integrity, he's always got your back.

THE SUNSHiNE MiND WAY TO . . .
WALK IN INTEGRITY

If you're in a situation where you're unsure of what God is calling you to do, here is a prayer to seek his guidance.

Dear Lord,
Please walk beside me as I navigate this situation. I am over-whelmed and unsure of what to do. Please help me not to react with emotion but rather the way you would in this circumstance. Guide my tongue as I speak, direct my feet as I move forward, and lead me to grace. In Jesus's name. Amen.

FiND SOLiTUDE

Very early in the morning, while it was still dark, Jesus got up, left the house and went off to a solitary place, where he prayed.

—MARK 1:35

Tanya

I can be especially hard on myself when I make simple mistakes. Slipups like forgetting birthdays, feeling like I dropped the ball by not being there for a friend, or even not paying parking tickets usually happen when I overbook myself. As a woman in the entertainment industry (who had been constantly plagued with imposter syndrome), I always felt I needed to prove myself and that saying no wasn't an option. I overpacked my schedule for years, and honestly, that allowed me to block out any discomfort or sadness in my personal life. When the pandemic hit and I was forced to slow way down, I felt anxious and overwhelmed. I shifted my focus from my usual work responsibilities and events to obsessing over every aspect of my life where I "hadn't reached my goals" yet. This changed my mood from the upbeat and bubbly Tanya everyone knew to gloomy and sullen. I knew I needed to be still. I knew I needed to be with God. So I started programming that time into my morning routine.

Whenever I feel overwhelmed, I put on worship music in my living room and sing at the top of my lungs. Worshiping in solitude can immediately bring peace to my day. Taking time to be alone and still, spending time solely with God, can take away all the anxiety, all the stress, and quickly bring me to a place of gratitude and love. Whenever you find yourself getting caught up in the craziness of your day-to-day life, remember this tip from Jesus: find solitude and pray!

Our lives can become hectic when we're constantly spinning on the hamster wheel of activity and don't feel like we're moving forward. Work commitments, birthday parties, family obligations, holidays, kids' activities, school events—the list can go on and on. We can spread ourselves so thin that we quickly lose focus. We start complaining about our laundry list of obligations instead of being grateful for all the amazing opportunities we've been given. We become stressed about our schedule or calendar and fail to see that God has blessed us with a career we're passionate about and people in our lives who make us a better version of ourselves. The words of Mark 1:35 remind us that when Jesus felt overwhelmed, he went off to a solitary place to pray.

THE SUNSHINE MIND WAY TO . . . FIND SOLITUDE

Today, carve out fifteen minutes to sit alone and write down a list of everything you are grateful for. Be specific. Be lighthearted. Be intentional. Take the entire fifteen minutes to do this. Set an alarm on your phone, and keep writing until the alarm goes off. As you make your list, envision those things you are grateful for. Thank God for bringing them into your life. The fifteen minutes might feel like an eternity at first because most of us aren't used to being still or in solitude, but trust us, it will be good for your soul.

LOVE OTHERS

Do not seek revenge or bear a grudge against anyone among your people, but love your neighbor as yourself. I am the Lord.

—LEVITICUS 19:18

Raquelle

Seeking revenge or holding a grudge is never the answer to a problem. It only stirs up more conflict. When a friend has hurt me, my initial reaction can be to withdraw or in the heat of the moment if they send a text message, it can be tempting to say something hurtful back. But I know deep down that this solves nothing. It takes more strength to say, "Hey, this hurt me and this is why . . ." than it does to ignore or retaliate. Think about how you would want someone to speak to you if you had done something hurtful. You would want them to tell you in a way that was truthful and loving, wouldn't you? Having a Sunshine Mind means communicating in a way that is vulnerable and real without seeking revenge or holding a grudge. When you react in the right way, it eliminates drama and allows you to love your neighbor as yourself.

The way you treat others is a reflection of how you think of yourself. The greatest indicator of self-love is treating others with love. But society tells us to do the opposite. We are encouraged to find entertainment in competitive shows where people cheat and argue, fighting with each other on-screen for an hour straight. (Hey, no shade to anyone who enjoys these shows. We, too, sometimes find this kind of TV entertaining.) Our culture teaches us that nastiness wins. But this isn't how God wants us to act. He wants us to love him, love ourselves, and then go and love others.

THE SUNSHINE MIND WAY TO . . . LOVE OTHERS

What you put into your life will eventually come out in the things you say and do. To live your best life and love others, look at what you're filling your life, and your heart, with:

- Be selective about what you're digesting on a regular basis. How can you change your media habits—shows, books, social media—to better reflect the way you want to live?
- Watch shows about people you truly admire, not about those you aspire to be like superficially.
- Follow influencers and friends on social media who spread kindness and positivity. Reflect this in your own social media feed.

HELP ONE ANOTHER

*You, my brothers and sisters, were called to be free.
But do not use your freedom to indulge the flesh;
rather, serve one another humbly in love.*

—GALATIANS 5:13

Tanya

In my neighborhood, I walk by many unhoused people hanging out on the street. Because I never carry cash anymore, I used to feel horrible, not having any money to give them. Then I realized that what might be even better than giving them cash would be providing food and encouragement. Raquelle and I came up with an idea. We filled brown paper bags with water, juice, granola bars, nuts, socks, toothbrushes—as much as we could stuff into each bag. We received such warm responses when we handed out these bags of love. And I can't express the feelings of love and deep gratitude we felt in our own souls in return.

The Sunshine Mind is all about loving and helping your neighbor. We've mentioned many times the importance of focusing on other people and being of service to them. That's because this is one of the surest ways to spread joy and light to others. Helping one another in love means accepting people exactly where they are and noticing when and where someone has a need. Those we spend the most time with will always be at the forefront of our thoughts, but thinking about those outside our circles is important too. When we pay attention to the details, like noticing a friend who seems down or the person at the coffee shop who could use some encouragement, we'll see that opportunities to spread love are all around us. Helping others should never be done from a point of superiority, of course. We all need love and help, even if our need is different than someone else's. When we understand the freedom we have in God's unconditional love, that frees us to go out and love others.

THE SUNSHINE MIND WAY TO . . .
HELP ONE ANOTHER

We want to encourage you to use some time this week to serve those who may be forgotten or overlooked. To make time, maybe save that new TV series you've been wanting to binge for another weekend, move a nail appointment back, or skip your weekly friend date. Or if you have plans with friends, see if they want to join you in helping others! Maybe your group could even make it a regular thing. However you do it, make it a priority this week to help someone you don't know.

BE THE DiFFERENCE

Gentle words are a tree of life;
a deceitful tongue crushes the spirit.

—PROVERBS 15:4 NLT

Tanya

I feel extremely lucky that most of the comments I receive on social media are positive and encouraging. I am usually disciplined about not reading comments on my podcast because outside opinions of me are none of my business. But one day I went in, and boy, was it damaging. Reading some of those reviews put me in a dark headspace. I couldn't even "Tanya" my way out of the dark clouds those reviews brought into my sunshine-filled day. People called me annoying and loud; it was a tough pill to swallow. Until I had a revelation: Yeah, I am those things. And I'm proud of it! I am uniquely made this way. Love it or leave it, baby. People like to complain more than they like to compliment. And I couldn't let these comments be my problem. God and my friends and those who love me tell me positive things about myself. Why should I listen to anyone else?

ometimes we don't give words enough credit. Remember the last time someone complimented you? How did that make you feel? If we realize the positive impact a compliment can make, why are we not giving them out like hotcakes? We want to encourage you to bring some gentle words to a dark place: social media. Go to your social media platform of choice (or every single one of them if you want extra credit!) and start spreading love and light with your words. Comment generously on pictures. Say kind words about what people are doing. Spread some positivity in a space that is often filled with sarcasm and darkness. Also take it beyond social media and write some positive Online reviews. Heck, go on and write some glowing reviews of your favorite podcasts or books. Let's be the bright spot. Let's be that ray of sunshine. Let's be the difference.

THE SUNSHINE MIND WAY TO . . . BE THE DIFFERENCE

This week, go out of your way to write positive comments on social media and give glowing reviews online. When commenting on social media, use the hashtag #SunshineMindBook so we can find your words of positivity and share them.

POSITIVE CHANGE CHALLENGE

- Fifteen encouraging comments on social media
- Five glowing reviews online
- One email to customer service praising something their establishment has done right

Day 37

GiVE LOVE AND GRACE

"Then neither do I condemn you,"
Jesus declared. "Go now and
leave your life of sin."

—JOHN 8:11

Tanya

In college I hooked up with a guy my good friend was really into. I'd had too much to drink and wasn't thinking about my actions or the consequences. But afterward the guilt was paralyzing. I felt terrible. I was accountable for my actions and apologized, hoping she would forgive me. But it forever altered my friendship with the girl and rightfully so. Every relationship is built on trust, and I lost hers. Fortunately, in time and through prayer, I forgave myself. This experience changed me. I resolved to never again pursue or even look at someone my friend has or had feelings for. Guys come and go. Friends are forever.

We are all flawed and destined to make mistakes. We let our friends down. We make poor decisions and slip up from time to time. We know something is wrong, but we do it anyway. Usually we feel shame about what we did. And sometimes we make someone else feel bad or guilty about what they did. But God wants to extend his grace and love to each of us. People will let you down. You will let people down too. But it's not on us to point the finger or cast the stone.

In the book of John, we find a story about a woman who has committed adultery. You can read the entire story in John 7:53–8:11, but in a nutshell, here's what happened: A group of scribes and Pharisees interrupted Jesus while he was teaching. They had brought with them this woman who had committed adultery, saying she should be stoned for what she did. Jesus said that anyone who hadn't sinned should throw the first stone. No one was eligible to cast a stone because they were all sinners. Jesus then said, I don't condemn you either. Go and sin no more. If Jesus had condemned this woman, she would have felt horrible and probably would have continued her poor behavior. But because Jesus extended grace and love to her, she was able to experience freedom from shame, and we believe she went on to become a better version of herself. This story is a great lesson and reminder for all of us. No matter what happens, it's not our job to judge. We're to be like Jesus, forgiving others and giving them—and ourselves—love and grace.

THE SUNSHINE MIND WAY TO . . . GIVE LOVE AND GRACE

When you're upset or disappointed in someone, communicate your feelings in a productive way. Maintain your grace by leading with love, not anger or passive aggressive behavior. Taking the high road can be difficult, especially when you're experiencing strong emotions. When you're ready, give that person love and grace, feel free to use these words as a suggestion: You hurt me, but I know we all make mistakes. I'm certainly not perfect, and I don't expect you to be either. I forgive you.

BE DONE WiTH SHAME

But the Lord God helps me;
therefore I have not been disgraced;
therefore I have set my face like a flint,
and I know that I shall not be put to shame.

—ISAIAH 50:7 ESV

Raquelle

I remember a time in high school when all my friends were invited to a party and I wasn't. It wasn't just a Friday night hang out kind of party. Invitations had been sent, a venue had been rented, and it was all everyone was talking about. The girl who didn't invite me wasn't someone I had any sort of issue with; nothing bad had happened between us. But for whatever reason, she didn't want to invite me. Naturally this made me wonder, "Is there something wrong with me? Am I not good enough?" If I let that shame sink into my soul, it could have made me insecure in future situations. There will always be times when we don't get the invite, don't get the job, the list goes on. We have to make a conscious effort to let go of shame, asking God to help us see ourselves as he sees us so that no person or situation can push us into a shame spiral.

One of our favorite authors, Brené Brown, talks about the difference between guilt and shame. She says that guilt is "I did something bad" while shame is "I am bad." That is a *huge* difference. Guilt can be a good thing because it helps us not to make the same bad choices in the future. But when we live in shame, we live in darkness. God doesn't shame us; therefore, we shouldn't shame ourselves. When we repent from our mistakes, we find forgiveness and freedom.

We love the story of the prodigal son (which you can read in Luke 15:11–32) because it's a great reminder of how much God loves us. In this story, the son asks for and receives a portion of his inheritance. Then he runs away and wastes all he has been given. Because of all the bad decisions he makes, he feels a lot of shame about what he's done and is scared to go back to his father. He feels he is no longer worthy to be called a son. But when he finally does build up the courage to go see his father, he is welcomed with compassion, open arms, and so much love. Like the prodigal son, we sometimes beat ourselves up about the decisions we've made and develop a sense of shame. And if we are living in shame, we can't live freely. When we repent, God forgives us immediately, wipes away all the bad things we have done, and welcomes us back with open arms.

THE SUNSHINE MIND WAY TO . . .
BE DONE WITH SHAME

When you feel shame about something, and feel like you are a bad person, pray this prayer to experience freedom:

Dear God,
I release [the thing you feel shame about] to you. I know you have not called me to live in shame but that you have forgiven me and want me to live in total freedom. Please help me not to focus on the past and the bad things I've done but instead to focus on the good and what is to come. Thank you for loving me, and help me to remember that shame can't exist in love. Help me also to extend this same love to others. Amen.

BUILD YOUR LiFE ON A STRONG FOUNDATION

"Everyone who hears these words of mine and puts them into practice is like a wise man who built his house on the rock. The rain came down, the streams rose, and the winds blew and beat against that house; yet it did not fall, because it had its foundation on the rock. But everyone who hears these words of mine and does not put them into practice is like a foolish man who built his house on sand. The rain came down, the streams rose, and the winds blew and beat against that house, and it fell with a great crash."

—MATTHEW 7:24-27

Raquelle

Sometimes life gets hard, and without a foundation rooted in faith, the storms that come our way will make us crumble. For example, all my work is project-based, so when one project ends, I don't always know when the next one will come. I have to trust that God will continue to open doors for the next right project. If I weren't rooted in my faith, I might live my entire life anxious about when the next project will come. Choosing to trust and rely on my faith as that solid foundation allows me to have peace in the waiting. We can apply this trust to all areas of our lives, from the really hard stuff to the small stuff, knowing that building our foundation on the Rock is one that can't be shaken.

The parable of the builders is a representation of two types of people—the wise and the foolish. The wise person builds their house on the rock. The foolish person builds their house on the sand. Building on the rock represents building a life on the teachings and wisdom of Jesus—forgiveness, taking the high road, compassion, patience, grace, self-control, kindness. Building on the sand represents the opposite—practicing unforgiveness, getting even, living life for yourself, making reckless decisions, using poor judgment. If built on sand, your house will eventually sink. When set on rock, you're steady and stable. We love this parable because it shows that living a life of wisdom requires a strong foundation. We have found that through the practice of the Sunshine Mind, we've been able to build a solid foundation for our lives.

THE SUNSHINE MIND WAY TO . . . BUILD YOUR LIFE ON A STRONG FOUNDATION

- Have faith in Jesus and in God's Word.
- Write down your daily and weekly goals.
- Treat your body well by making healthy choices.
- Surround yourself with happy, honest, and loyal people.
- Be generous with your time, talents, and possessions.

SHARE, DON'T COMPARE

"Be on your guard against all kinds of greed; life does not consist in an abundance of possessions."

Tanya

My coworker Ryan Seacrest is someone I admire very much. I will never forget the day I met him, my very first day on the job. He greeted me with the warmest welcome and made me feel part of the family right from the start. People always ask me what it's like working with him, and to me, the proof is in the pudding. I've worked alongside him for over a decade now and wouldn't want it any other way. Not only is this a dream job for me, but working alongside someone with so much passion, so much purpose, and such strong character (and—I'll admit it only in this book—truly one of the funniest people I've ever known) is the biggest blessing.

Ryan has worked extremely hard to get where he is today. He has faced rejection and gotten up time and time again. He has blazed new trails in the entertainment industry and is a man many people look up to. I truly believe his greatest fulfillment comes from the work he does through his foundation, the Ryan Seacrest Foundation.

This foundation builds broadcast media centers in pediatric hospitals so patients can be creative and explore radio, television, and new media. This helps contribute to the healing process for children and their families during their stays at the hospital.

Raquelle and I have spent a lot of time at the RSF studio inside Children's Hospital of Orange County. Once a month we would spend time in the studio talking, playing bingo, and getting relationship advice from our favorite sixteen-year-old patient, who was a God-gift to us all. We saw firsthand the community, the laughter, and the light these studios create inside the walls of the hospital.

I believe Ryan would say this accomplishment has brought him the most fulfillment in his life and career because it is focused entirely on helping others.

The parable of the rich fool (which you can read in Luke 12:13–21) is a great reminder that true wealth comes from helping others and we shouldn't get caught up in our own possessions and successes. In the parable, the rich man has an abundance of crops. His solution? Build bigger barns to store his harvest! In doing so, he focuses only on himself and loses sight of helping the people around him. In this digital age, we constantly get an inside look at other people's lives—and some of them look a lot like the rich fool. And when we see that others have what we don't, sometimes we play the comparison game. We might think that having the biggest and the best leads to a happy and fulfilled life, but it doesn't. It usually leads to quite the opposite. Sharing, not obsessing over, our possessions is what we are called to do. Trying to accumulate riches only for yourself leads to a miserable life. Being in the entertainment industry, we have seen that firsthand. Unless you use your platform and resources to enhance the lives of others, it will never satisfy.

THE SUNSHINE MIND WAY TO . . .
SHARE, DON'T COMPARE

Sharing with others is one of the best ways to show God's love. What are some causes you care about? How can you get involved in one of those causes today? Whether you donate money, volunteer your time, or commit to pray daily for those who lead that organization, God will bless your efforts.

Day 41

PRACTICE POSITIVE SELF-TALK

*She is clothed with strength and dignity;
she can laugh at the days to come.*

Tanya and Raquelle

We have a good friend, we'll call her Kim, who up until recently worked for an extremely difficult person. Kim's boss was well known and powerful, the kind of person who could make anything happen, good or bad, with one phone call. Kim was motivated by the opportunity to work for someone so influential and wanted to do well at her job. The problem was, her boss was crazy mean! She often derailed Kim from doing a good job by being cruel and demeaning. She yelled a lot, calling Kim "stupid" or "dumb." At first Kim would sneak away to cry and question herself: "Am I really that stupid?" But after checking in with us and other friends, she realized she didn't get to where she was by being dumb. So one day she put into practice what we'll call "shade shielding." She used her inner light to counter the darkness her boss threw at her. When her boss began a tirade, Kim would tell herself, "I am a good person. I always help others. I am creative and witty. I love to make others laugh." She learned to make her inner voice louder than the one trying to tear her down. Although this tactic worked, Kim left her job and found herself in a much better place. God had bigger plans for her but first wanted her to learn to love herself.

We believe in the power of repetition. Have you ever practiced an instrument or a sport and, after a couple of lessons, started getting the hang of it? The same is true with positive self-talk. Practice makes perfect, and the more you speak kindly about yourself, the more you will truly believe it. And then it becomes second nature. Remember, you are a strong woman. You are "clothed with strength and dignity" (Proverbs 31:25).

THE SUNSHINE MIND WAY TO . . . PRACTICE POSITIVE SELF-TALK

While looking in a mirror, speak each sentence of the following affirmation. Look yourself in the eye and mean every single word you say.

I look in the mirror today and see a strong human:

- A human who used to focus on their flaws but now finds strengths.
- A confident human who makes everyone feel included and welcome.
- A human who leads with love.
- A human who doesn't shy away from difficulties.
- A human who perseveres.
- A human who chooses to find the good.
- A human who brings light and positivity to the world.
- Sunshine in human form.

PRIORITIZE CHARACTER OVER CHEMISTRY

Consider it pure joy, my brothers and sisters, whenever you face trials of many kinds, because you know that the testing of your faith produces perseverance. Let perseverance finish its work so that you may be mature and complete, not lacking anything.

—JAMES 1:2-4

Tanya

My friend Ben Higgins—you may have seen him on a little show called *The Bachelor*—is a man of integrity and character. It was at his wedding where I heard the pastor speak about the importance of prioritizing character over chemistry. This concept seems obvious, but I'd never thought of it this way. I used to prioritize chemistry over character. I would let that "spark" or physical connection drown out any obvious red flags or disconnections. Today, I know you can have character and chemistry together in a perfect combo. So focus on who your man is at his core—his morals, his values, how he treats people, how he treats you, how he wants to help others and the world. That's the good stuff right there.

Character over chemistry. Always. In the dating world, especially on the apps, you lead with chemistry. Whose photos are you attracted to? Who do you click with most over text? Is there a "spark" when you meet in real life? At the beginning of relationships, we can focus so much on the chemistry that we lose sight of the more important C word: character. Chemistry fades. Chemistry can give you a good relationship for a hot minute, but it's only temporary, whether it's a few weeks or a few years. But character lasts a lifetime. If you are dating someone with good character, that is the person you should focus on.

It's human nature to be influenced by the law of chemistry. But if we let chemistry override the importance of someone's character, we can end up in a situation that's extremely dissatisfying in virtually every way. When James 1:4 says, "Be mature and complete, not lacking anything," it means when we live our lives maturely or with good character, we gain wisdom and lack nothing.

THE SUNSHINE MIND WAY TO . . . PRIORITIZE CHARACTER OVER CHEMISTRY

Early on, I was a big "lists girl" when it came to dating. Everyone told me, "You want a man? Write down what you want—and be specific!" And boy was I specific. My lists were always a bit shallow: nice hair, six feet tall, dresses well, easy on the eyes, and never orders a drink with a straw. My lists focused on chemistry over character. When I had this pivotal shift in my thinking and realized what I really wanted, my "list" became more of a prayer. God, I want a life partner who sees me as an equal. I want a man who will lead our family. I want a loyal man, a man of his word. I want a teammate who will lift me up when I'm down and acknowledge achievements I make both personally and professionally. I want a partner who doesn't take himself too seriously. I want a love where I can place my heart in his hand and have full faith that he will protect it and care for it. When my prayers were focused on this person's character, God showed me the way and gave me a new level of discernment that I had lacked in my dating life.

Day 43

FiND LiGHT IN THE DARKNESS

Thou tellest my wanderings:
put thou my tears into thy bottle: are
they not in thy book?

—PSALM 56:8 KJV

Raquelle

A few years ago I had to trust God and find his light in the darkness when a friend of mine was severely struggling mentally. I felt helpless as nothing I could say or do would change what she was going through. This is someone very important to me, and it was devastating to know she was potentially not going to come out of the state she was in. I still remember going to visit her, and when I left, I sobbed, asking God why. The situation was so hard for me that I spent a lot of time in prayer and worship; it was the only thing that helped during that dark time. Thank God she did get better, and I now look back on that time and am so grateful for how God healed my friend and for how I experienced comfort even in the darkness.

There is no real understanding of why bad things happen to good people, why people get sick, or why there are wars. We live in a broken world, but despite this we always have the peace of eternity to look forward to. John 16:33 says, "In this world you will have trouble. But take heart! I have overcome the world." Many of the bad things in this world will never make sense to us, but in heaven we will have total peace, all pain will be gone, and we will live in perfect unity with God and each other. Until then, when the dark times come, we can rely on the Lord as our refuge. We won't always understand why something bad has happened, but we can find comfort in the fact that God sees every tear. His presence is the ultimate comfort in the midst of circumstances that often make no sense. Whatever you are facing today, God says that if you seek him, you will find him (Luke 11:10). In the midst of your tears, seek him, cry out to him, and he will meet you exactly where you are.

THE SUNSHINE MIND WAY TO . . . FIND LIGHT IN THE DARKNESS

When you're struggling to make sense of a situation and need comfort, pray this prayer:

Dear God,
Please guide me to the meaning behind this situation. For I know you have a plan and a purpose. Your plan is never to hurt me but to prosper me. Open my eyes to what you are teaching me at this moment. Open my heart to receive the good that will come from this situation. I know storms don't last forever. Please protect me in this time of need. Amen.

MAKE IT THROUGH HEARTBREAK

*He heals the brokenhearted
and binds up their wounds.*

—PSALM 147:3

Tanya

Are you going through heartbreak right now? Girl, let me tell you—I feel you. The life of a hopeful romantic can feel brutal at times. (Yes, I use the term *hopeful* romantic instead of *hopeless* romantic because that's part of having a Sunshine Mind.) We hopeful romantics relate to Taylor Swift songs a little *too* much, we cry at any romantic gesture in a movie, on TV, or even on social media, and we wear our hearts on our sleeves. But having this type of heart is beautiful. God made this heart specifically and wonderfully yours. Don't let your hopes fade or your heart grow cold through any heartbreak. It's a blessing to be able to experience the peaks and even the valleys. Don't think of your heartbreak as having to "start all over again . . . ugh," but see it as an opportunity to learn from your past and become a better partner in the future. (I say this because relationships don't usually end because of the actions of only one person, but rather a combined effort on both accounts. Take responsibility for your shortcomings, and be stronger in those areas next time around.) The Bible promises that God will heal the brokenhearted. Look to him.

When your heart has been shattered, trust that God will fulfill the desires of your heart. You might feel broken right now, but God has a perfect plan waiting for you. As you let go of the broken relationship, realize God may have brought this person into your life to teach you something, and open your heart to understanding and appreciating the purpose behind this relationship. Then pray for your future partner. Pray for their heartbreak or anything they might be going through right now. Pray that everything will make sense when the two of you meet. God will heal your broken heart. He will also fulfill your heart's desires, and he will do that in his divine timing.

THE SUNSHINE MIND WAY TO . . . MAKE IT THROUGH HEARTBREAK

If you need a heartbreak bestie, let us be that for you because matters of the heart cut deep . . . don't we know it. There is no "one size fits all" when it comes to heartbreak. What works for someone might sound like torture to you and that's okay. It's about listening to *your* heart and going at *your* speed and not about following a specific blueprint. However, here are some recommendations of practices that have helped me, and hopefully they can help you too.

> **SOCIAL DETOX**. Why are you waiting to hit Unfollow? This isn't a petty move, this is a protecting move. Out of sight out of mind. Don't worry about what the other person will think. This will be good for your heart and mind.
>
> **WORK OUT**. Elle Woods was onto something when she said, "Endorphins make you happy. Happy people just don't kill their husbands, they just don't."[2] When you

exercise, your body releases endorphins, which trigger a positive feeling—it's just the facts. If you don't enjoy running, go on walks. If you hate cardio, try yoga. Intimidated by big group classes? Videos on YouTube and many at-home apps allow you to work out in the privacy of your own home. Commit to being active every day; it will bring the sunshine in many ways.

PURGE AND HIDE. I'm not saying to throw away everything this person ever gave you or anything that reminds you of them. I'm saying put it all in one place, maybe in the back of a closet. Don't torture yourself with looking at these things and reminding yourself of what "once was."

WRITE. How many of you have left a relationship but still wanted closure? Closure is something you have to find within yourself because talking in circles will get you nowhere. Sometimes a relationship simply doesn't work—and that's okay. Maybe you were cheated on and deserve an apology that you never got. Seeking closure from someone who has broken your heart is a double-edged sword. Instead, write a lengthy letter of everything you would want to say to them. You're not actually going to give it to that person but rather keep it for yourself (or burn it). Just the process of getting those thoughts out of your head and onto paper can help immeasurably.

SURROUND. Surround yourself with fun and friends and family. Let their positivity bring you light. Enjoy their love and soak it all in.

Day 45

BE PATIENT WITH LOVE

Love is patient and kind; love does not envy or boast; it is not arrogant or rude.

–1 CORINTHIANS 13:4-5 ESV

Tanya

When I met the man of my dreams, we were in very different phases of life. I was ready for marriage, kids, all the things—and I wanted them yesterday. And let's just say he was . . . not exactly in the same life phase. The first phase of our journey was slower than I would have wanted or pictured, but Raquelle reminded me of this exact Bible passage any time I would come to her in a tizzy. (She has reminded me of these verses more times than you can imagine. Hey, I'm not perfect, but I try hard. I just need reminders every once in a while.) I was able to pull myself together and be patient. And it was worth it. I have an awesome partner in my boyfriend. So let this be an encouragement to any of you who are feeling impatient in your pursuit of love. We are all on different journeys, and being patient with each other is the best way to get to the right place.

The first words this passage uses to describe love are "love is patient." *Sayyy whaaa?* For me, who grew up on Disney movies, I (Tanya!) would have said love is bliss, love is wonderful, love is magical. But *patient*? This never made sense to me. I built my career on being impatient. Everything in our society has been shifting quickly toward instant gratification. You want your favorite meal from across town? Uber Eats. Need someone to fix your mirror? TaskRabbit. Don't want to drive? Uber. Heck, even our hearts expect instant gratification. You want a date tonight? Tinder! But true love—the partner-you've-always-dreamed-of kind of love—takes patience. The Supremes were on to something when they said, "You can't hurry love; no, you just have to wait." Being patient in love means giving the other person grace and room to grow and thrive on their own personal path. Love is a lot of things, but first of all, love is patient.

THE SUNSHINE MIND WAY TO . . . BE PATIENT WITH LOVE

Patience has been the hardest practice for me to learn. Here are a couple of practices that have helped me.

> **IDENTIFY.** Figure out where the impatience is coming from. Is the stage you wish you were in right now truly a desire of your heart? Or is it something society says you should be doing?
>
> **ACCEPT YOUR CURRENT SITUATION.** You might not be exactly where you want to be, but you are definitely on the way. Live day by day and try to live in the moment.
>
> **IT'S OKAY TO FEEL UNCOMFORTABLE.** You probably aren't going to be happy in every single season of life, and

that's okay. Accept the discomfort and live in the moment.

BECOME A LISTENER. It's easy to constantly talk about and stew in the negativity. Instead, practice the art of listening. Ask about where your friends are in life, listen to some educational podcasts, or call someone and listen to what's happening in their life.

MEDITATE AND BE STILL. Patience comes from a place of calmness and peace. Try sitting still and focusing on your breathing.

PRACTICE PATIENCE

Whoever is patient has great understanding,
but one who is quick-tempered displays folly.

—PROVERBS 14:29

Raquelle

I once heard that patience is the key to contentment. I've thought a lot about this because having patience is a daily challenge for all of us. Work situations are an area where patience can be tough for me. Often I am working with many different personality types, and though I know it's extremely important to be able to work with people who work differently than me, this requires patience. Something that has helped me with this is knowing that sometimes there isn't a right or wrong way to get something done; everyone is just different so I can be patient knowing that my way isn't necessarily the only right way. Taking a deep breath during impatient moments and looking at things from a 360 perspective has helped me greatly when it comes to having patience, and ultimately how we make people feel and showing God's kindness is always the way to go instead of being frustrated and impatient which only leads to folly like Proverbs 14:29 says.

Patience can apply to everyday events such as traffic and being on time for meetings, but it also applies to more complex parts of life like wellness and relationships. For example, we need to be patient with people and accept them for who they are and where they're at. If we spend our time getting frustrated and impatient with others, we can miss out on a beautiful connection. The Bible talks a lot about patience because practicing it is key to living a peaceful life. And I (Raquelle) believe it talks so much about it because it isn't easy; it requires surrendering to God's timing versus our timing. Opportunities to practice patience show up every day. When impatient thoughts come, like, "Why is this traffic not moving?" I find it helpful to embrace the moment by listening to music or a podcast, realizing that the traffic is out of my control. Or if a relationship isn't moving as quickly as I would like, I pray for the person instead of pushing them too fast into something they might not be ready for. If, instead, I start honking my horn or cutting people off in traffic, I can make others angry and solve nothing, or get a ticket. And if I try to push someone into something they aren't ready for (this applies to all types of relationships), I could end up ruining the relationship entirely.

A big part of living the Sunshine Mind way is practicing patience so we can be content with all life throws our way.

THE SUNSHINE MIND WAY TO . . .
PRACTICE PATIENCE

When you're stuck in traffic or feeling impatient with someone, say this prayer as a way of practicing patience:

Dear God,
I'm seeking your patience today. Please settle my feelings of restlessness. Help me to let go of the things I can't control, and help me to be content while waiting. Take away any anxious feelings I have. I know everything happens in your divine timing, and I trust you, Lord. Amen.

Day 47

WATCH YOUR WORDS

May these words of my mouth and this
meditation of my heart
be pleasing in your sight,
LORD, my Rock and my Redeemer.

—PSALM 19:14

Raquelle

I have a friend who, for weeks on end every time we would talk, had something negative or unkind to say about something or someone. I became frustrated, and it got to the point where I was about to say something harsh in regard to the negativity. I got off the phone with her one day and felt God speaking to me, telling me that this friend was being negative and unkind because life—and the people in it—had recently been unkind to her in many ways. I decided I would be kind and empathetic the next time we spoke, and my friend's tone completely changed after I did this. If I had chosen to respond to her harshly, it would only have added to the negativity and made it worse. This has been a good lesson that my own response can change a situation.

W ords are containers for power. They carry either creative power or destructive power."[3] I love this quote by Joyce Meyer. Words are powerful. They can change an atmosphere, change a perspective, even change a life. Words have the power to stir up anger and negativity or bring gentleness and positivity. Always be mindful of the power your words carry. Let them shine light into other people's lives, even during anger and conflict. Your response has the power to change the entire situation—and change someone's life.

THE SUNSHINE MIND WAY TO . . . WATCH YOUR WORDS

Often the problem is not the message but rather the delivery. Next time you're tempted to respond harshly, put your words through a softening filter before releasing them. Never respond out of emotion. You may have a favorite filter for photos. Pick your favorite filter for your words:

- Process with a levelheaded friend.
- Sleep on it.
- Respond first in your notes app rather than texting right away.
- Consider where the other person is coming from.
- Run your response by a trusted friend or coworker first.

Day 48

GET STRONGER

She sets about her work vigorously;
her arms are strong for her tasks.

—PROVERBS 31:17

Tanya

I know I am at my best when I am strength training and moving my body regularly. It makes everyday tasks easier without me even realizing it. Whenever I'm preparing for a big event, like a red carpet, I make it a point to do something physical every day beforehand, no matter how busy my schedule is. This isn't for vanity purposes, it's for mental purposes. I've noticed I can work harder and be sharper and that my daily tasks are more manageable when my body is used to movement. Being physically strong always has a positive effect not only on my body but also on my mind, helping me feel mentally strong enough to take on whatever comes my way.

In Proverbs 31:17 God isn't saying a woman needs to hit the gym to get strong. But he is saying that a woman needs to find strength within her for her life tasks. Like physical strength, inner strength can build up over time. Strength is built when we lean on God during tough times. God never throws anything our way that we can't handle—rather he constantly challenges us to make us stronger.

THE SUNSHINE MIND WAY TO . . . GET STRONGER

- If you aren't really a workout person, try walking. Instead of catching up with a friend over dinner and drinks, go for a walk together.
- Sign up to be a dog walker (a side hustle that gives you some extra cash while getting you in shape. It's a win-win, baby!). Or donate your time at an animal shelter and walk the dogs there.
- Set your alarm for fifteen minutes earlier every morning so you can meditate.
- Look at your daily schedule and figure out where you can squeeze in some extra activity.
- Need us to hold you accountable? Use the hashtag #SunshineMindBook to let us know what you're doing. We will be your besties and help push you along in your strength and fitness journey.

OPEN YOUR HEART

Every animal of the forest is Mine,
The cattle on a thousand hills.
I know every bird of the mountains,
And everything that moves in the field is Mine.

—PSALM 50:10–11 NASB

Tanya

When I first got my puppy, my entire routine was thrown off. Forget moving my body daily—I didn't do anything physical for weeks. The puppy woke me up every two hours throughout the night, so I was sluggish during the day and foggy at work. I wasn't the best Tanya when it came to any of my relationships because I was giving less to my coworkers and not seeing my friends as much. My life was off-balance, but it was okay because it was temporary. After a couple of weeks, my sweet Sunny girl was sleeping through the night, and I got back to my pre-zombie, Tanya-vibe life. After I came out of my sleepless, foggy state, I quickly realized that my pre-puppy life had been missing something—the unconditional, lights-up-the-room, all-consuming love that had entered my life in the shape of a sweet Cavapoo puppy. She brought a new type of love into my life that I don't believe any human could. Animals bring peace, animals bring stillness, animals bring light.

Opening your heart to an animal can bring peace, joy, and love to your soul. All that little animal wants to do is love unconditionally and asks for nothing in return. But an animal's love doesn't compare to the greatest example of unconditional love—the love of God. He extends his love and grace to us as a gift. Even when we sin, God is standing there with his arms open wide, ready to forgive us. This type of love is selfless, unconditional, and all-consuming.

THE SUNSHINE MIND WAY TO . . . OPEN YOUR HEART

Have you been thinking about bringing an animal into your life? (Did I convince you to take the plunge? Or maybe scare you off?) If getting a dog feels too overwhelming (and I hear that), here are some other suggestions:

- Adopt a smaller animal (bunny, hamster, kitten).
- Build a bird feeder in your backyard.
- Foster a puppy.
- Look after a friend's dog to give them a weekend off from puppy parent duties.
- Volunteer at an animal shelter.
- Donate to a charity that helps animals.

BE FINANCIALLY FIT

Let no debt remain outstanding, except the continuing debt to love one another, for whoever loves others has fulfilled the law.

—ROMANS 13:8

Tanya

When I first started working and earning money in high school, I thought that once my paycheck hit my bank account, it was time to spend it, baby! Commercials were always encouraging me to go out and spend my hard-earned money as soon as that direct deposit came through. Fortunately, my mom has always been financially savvy. Even when I was younger, I was blown away by her knowledge, especially because she came to this country as an immigrant who didn't even speak the language. My mom was a modern woman before I even knew what that term meant. She is the one who instilled in me the importance of saving, investing, and having my money work for me. Working smarter, not harder. She had spent too much of her life working in a corporate job that chewed her up and spit her out. (Don't even get me started on this rant 'cuz oh, momma, I could go off!) She would not allow that to happen to her children. I'm so grateful she taught me about money management skills because I have learned how to be financially fit and live a life that isn't plagued by financial stress, anxiety, or debt.

Let's focus on the beginning of Romans 13:8: "Let no debt remain outstanding." Our society has become so focused on what our lives look like on social media that we go to extremes to "keep up." Living at home with our parents rent-free so we can drive an expensive car. Maxing out credit cards to buy the new bag everyone is carrying. Booking luxurious trips instead of putting money toward paying off student loans. I (Tanya) can't express enough that imbalance with your finances will not stay contained to that one area of your life. The imbalance will create instability, anxiety, and stress, which will lead to sleep deprivation, which will impact your work and relationships—all of which will become a vicious cycle. The mental health benefits of being financially free isn't talked about enough. We glamorize unattainable lifestyles, and we go into debt to obtain them. But this is not the way of the Sunshine Mind. And it's not the way God would have us handle our finances. Make smart decisions with your money. The other areas of your life depend on it.

THE SUNSHINE MIND WAY TO . . .
BE FINANCIALLY FIT

Save your money. Don't keep up with the Joneses. You do you. What are some ways you can chip away at any debt you may have? Think about your current spending habits. Can you make any cuts? Can you take a portion of each paycheck—even a very small amount—and put it toward decreasing your debt?

Other tools we suggest:

> **APP.** Mint is a user-friendly app that can help you (a) create budgets, (b) get your free credit score, and (c) track your spending so you have a better picture of where your money is going.
> **BOOK.** *We Should All Be Millionaires* by Rachel Rodgers
> **PODCAST.** *Money Rehab with Nicole Lapin*

WORSHIP

The whole earth is filled with awe at your wonders; where morning dawns, where evening fades, you call forth songs of joy.

—PSALM 65:8

Raquelle

During a hard time in my life, worship helped me. Tanya and I had grown close to Moises, one of the teenagers we worked with during our time spent volunteering with the Ryan Seacrest Foundation. Moises was a patient at Children's Health of Orange County, and he was such a special soul. We built a relationship with him over the years, talking about our love lives, what we had done over the weekend, what our hopes were for the future. When we lost Moises, we were devastated. Worship brought both Tanya and me such comfort, knowing that our souls are forever and that one day we would be reunited with our friend. When we don't understand life, worship can help give us a peace that transcends our circumstances.

In the best of times, the worst of times, and everything in between, worship is our favorite thing. When we are in seasons of joy and abundance, thanking God for all the blessings in our lives, we are filled with awe and wonder. When we are in the darkest and worst of times, worship is a safe place of comfort. And when we are in the middle and stuck in the mundane, worship inspires us to be creative and in awe of who God is. Find some time to spend in worship today, and focus on something you want to thank God for, something you need comfort for, and something you want fresh passion for. As you shift your focus to God and his goodness, allow him to fill you with the incredible awe and wonder that worship can bring.

THE SUNSHINE MIND WAY TO . . . WORSHIP

Try incorporating these practices into your routine for one week and see what benefits they bring:

- Start your morning off by playing an uplifting worship song. This sets the tone for a peaceful start to whatever the day brings.
- End your day by listening to a worship song while thanking God for the good things that happened during the day.

Using these to practice allows us to start and end the day peacefully in worship. We have found that whatever we are facing—good, bad, and everything in between—worship changes everything.

Day 52

LEARN TO LOVE YOUR BODY

No one ever hated their own body, but they feed and care for their body, just as Christ does the church.

—EPHESIANS 5:29

Tanya

Have you ever hated your own body? 'Cuz I know I have. I have obsessed over the pouch under my tummy, working relentlessly to get rid of it. I have fixated on the cellulite on the backs of my legs. I have cried over certain pictures of myself. I have starved myself. I have tried every fad diet under the sun. I have had this up-and-down relationship with my body since I was in high school. I can confidently say that after daily practices and a healthy balance of admiration for my body and taking care of it, I have come to a place where I can say I love this body God gave me. I am unique. You won't find my body anywhere else in the world—'cuz it's mine. Is it perfect? No. Am I perfect? Definitely not. So why would I expect my body to be? When I began my bodylicious love journey, I placed sticky notes with positive affirmations all over my apartment as reminders to love myself and the God who made me. And I just kept adding to them.

Our bodies, whatever shapes or sizes, were given to us by God, uniquely chosen for our time on this earth. The same way God cherishes the church, we are to cherish our bodies and take care of ourselves. For us to live out each day secure in who God created us to be, we need to continually come against negative self-talk and replace our thoughts with the knowledge that God cherishes us. The following is a prayer you can pray when those thoughts come.

Lord,
As the Bible says, please help me to cherish my body the way you cherish the church. When insecurities come, I pray that you would replace those thoughts with your thoughts. Amen.

THE SUNSHINE MIND WAY TO . . .
LEARN TO LOVE YOUR BODY

Leave yourself love notes! Put them in your bathroom, inside your closet, or on the fridge. Find spaces where you can place these reminders and keep the love coming. Flooding your space with these affirmations combats negative self-talk and the comparison game you play on social media.

Some of our favorite self-love notes:

- You are perfectly made!
- My favorite part of my body is _____.
- I am proud of my ability to _____.
- I'm so fortunate to have beautiful _____.

Day 53

GET RiD OF RESENTMENT

Get rid of all bitterness, rage and anger, brawling and slander, along with every form of malice.

—EPHESIANS 4:31

Raquelle

In friendships where I haven't kept healthy boundaries, I have often felt resentment build up. If I'd just gone above and beyond for a friend, putting off my own needs, I feel frustrated when they ask me to help them with something else. It's not their fault, though. I'm the one who puts myself in this position by not saying anything about my full plate, explaining that I feel overwhelmed as is, or setting a boundary in our friendship and sticking to it. I think women are natural givers and caretakers, so where do we draw the line? I've often thought about Mark 12:31, which says to "love your neighbor as yourself." If we are giving to the point where we neglect ourselves, we aren't loving ourselves and therefore can't love our neighbor properly. So I have found that when resentment creeps in, it's because I have neglected some of my own needs. It's a hard balance, especially when you care about someone, but we have to make sure we take care of and love ourselves so that we can love others free from resentment.

The definition of *resentment* is bitterness toward being treated unfairly. This definition is interesting because it's a fact of life that sometimes people will treat us in a way that feels unfair. Resentment is one of those feelings that can creep up without warning. We might not even realize the feeling has been building up, and suddenly when someone says or does something, we feel anger and bitterness and resentment toward them, seemingly out of nowhere. Resentment can fracture relationships, which is why we need to get rid of it. The best way to do that is similar to letting go of unforgiveness—you have to give it to God, but you also need to process it internally for yourself, then release it and move forward.

Ultimately resentment comes from a lack of communication: when you don't communicate your expectations, when you don't communicate your needs, when you don't communicate that your feelings are being hurt. Over time, this lack of communication can cause resentment to build up.

THE SUNSHINE MIND WAY TO . . . GET RID OF RESENTMENT

You know the saying: holding on to resentment is like drinking poison and hoping the other person gets sick. Letting go isn't easy, but it's important not to hold on to that toxicity. Here are our tips for mentally moving forward.

WRITE IT OUT. Write a letter getting all your emotions out, then delete, burn, or rip it up.

FIND FORGIVENESS. Even if you don't make up, find space for forgiveness—if only for yourself.

SEEK HEALING. Speak to a therapist or pastor to mentally find your way out.

COMMUNICATE. Talk things through with the other person; be open and honest. Don't speak with your emotions in the heat of the moment. Rather, reflect on what it is that is hurting or bothering you, and think of proactive ways to approach it with someone.

APPROACH. Approach is key when communicating. Don't attack or blame the other person. Rather, acknowledge your negative or hurt feelings and consider proactive ways to combat them. Put yourself in the other person's shoes.

EXPECT NOTHING. Unmet expectations lead to disappointment.

BOUNDARIES ARE YOUR BFF. Boundaries are key to every relationship. You can't control other people, and you certainly can't control situations and circumstances, but you can control how people and circumstances impact your life. You can set boundaries to make sure people treat you with respect, and you can set boundaries as to how much you let situations and circumstances impact your mood.

Day 54

APPRECIATE YOUR SEASON

Give thanks in all circumstances; for this is God's will for you in Christ Jesus.

—1 THESSALONIANS 5:18

Tanya

For many years I had the job of my dreams and yet would focus on the love that was missing in my life. I was reaching career milestones but focusing on the bachelorette party or baby shower I wasn't having. I will never forget going through a breakup during this time and feeling so broken. I had a "Tanya day," where I ran for miles listening to modern-woman anthems. You know the ones: Kelly Clarkson's "Since U Been Gone," Beyonce's "Single Ladies." I cleaned my house, organized every cabinet, went on Instagram and shared my day in detail. I'll never forget a message a woman sent me in response to my post. She said, "I would give *anything* to have a day like yours. I'm currently typing this while potty training one kid, breastfeeding another, and cooking every meal for my husband, who can't lift a finger in the kitchen. Enjoy every minute of it!" Here was a woman who had everything I'd always wanted—the husband, the kids, the family—and she was messaging me about wanting to live *my* life for a day.

I realized that I needed to stop focusing on what I'd thought was greener grass. Once I shifted my mindset to focus on the positives of the life season I was in, I unlocked true happiness. I started appreciating that season for all the good it had to offer. I started enjoying waking up

113

whenever I wanted to on the weekends. I sprawled out and took up my entire bed because I could. I went out when I wanted to, stayed in when I wanted to. I soaked it all up because I knew that season wouldn't last forever. Now, as I sit here and write this, my season has changed drastically—in the best way. I wake up early on the weekends to take my angel puppy out to pee. I share my life with a wonderful partner who has two sweet little ones, and our weekends are filled with movie nights under a fort, cookie decorating parties, and kids' sports. Even though my life is still my own, I have obligations outside of myself that take my time—and I wouldn't want it any other way.

We often take the blessings we have for granted and forget to be thankful for what we have right now. Wishing we were in a different season of life and constantly thinking about what we don't have makes it hard to appreciate our current season. But someday we'll find ourselves in a different season, and we'll look back and miss the beauty and blessings of the season we were in. Next time you look at someone else's life and wish it were yours, remember that other people look at your life and wish the same thing. Be thankful in all circumstances and in all seasons of life. There is beauty right where you are.

THE SUNSHINE MIND WAY TO . . . APPRECIATE YOUR SEASON

Fill in the following blanks. Repeat these statements out loud every time you need to remember to appreciate your season.

I want _____, but I'm grateful I'm able to have _____ right now.

I may not have _____, but at least I'm able
    to _____.
There is blessing in this season of life because I get
    to _____.
God is blessing me in this season with the gift
    of _____.

PRAY BiG

Pray in the Spirit on all occasions with all kinds of prayers and requests. With this in mind, be alert and always keep on praying for all the Lord's people.

—EPHESIANS 6:18

Raquelle

My prayer life is one of the most important areas of my life. I spend a lot of time praying alone and also spend time praying with other people. Many of my friends ask me for prayer when they need it or I will offer it, and I consider that such a blessing. Often people are going through tough situations, and there aren't always answers to what they are facing or words to make it better. That is when I rely on the power of prayer, allowing God to use me as a vessel and inviting his presence. Never take this privilege for granted, and always direct them to the light of Jesus.

During hard moments I often call a family friend, Margaret, to pray for me. I have known her my entire life, and she is always happy and willing to pray for me no matter the circumstance. Prayer doesn't necessarily change a circumstance, but I always feel more peaceful afterward. The fact that she takes the time to pray is a reminder to me to do the same for others because I know how much comfort and help it has brought to me.

I do my best to show my friends that I love them unconditionally, free from any judgment, in the same way Margaret does for me. When you love people and show them that you are a trusted, safe place for them, they will likely accept your prayers and be directed to the light of Jesus.

God calls us to pray. When we pray, we are bringing our requests to him and lifting up ourselves, our family, our friends, and anyone else who has needs. Prayer is important because it brings us closer to God and to others. God always hears our prayers, and he always answers them. What a gift that is! It's important to pray not only for what we want in life and what others want but also for things outside our circle as well. Pray for people you don't know. Pray for other countries. Pray for peace in this broken world. Pray for anything God puts on your heart. Bring all kinds of prayers and requests to God, and don't be afraid to pray big.

THE SUNSHINE MIND WAY TO . . . PRAY BIG

Pray for five people today. Think outside the immediate circle of people you normally pray for. (You can keep praying for them, of course! But add those five new people to your list for today.) Pray for comfort. Pray for peace. Pray for clarity. Pray for healing. Pray big.

Day 56

HELP YOURSELF

Where there is no guidance, a people falls, but in an abundance of counselors there is safety.

—PROVERBS 11:14 ESV

Tanya

I pride myself on having a Sunshine Mind. I look at the positive side of any obstacle that comes my way. I try to seek solutions and answers instead of focusing on problems. But I reached a point in my life when I realized I was jamming my daily schedule so tight as an escape from some suppressed trauma I was holding on to from my childhood. We all have scarring moments in our pasts, whether we are aware of them or not. I never would have discovered mine had I not begun therapy at the start of the pandemic. When COVID hit and we were on lockdown, we were forced to slow down. I didn't know how to function without a jam-packed schedule. I wasn't comfortable sitting alone with my thoughts. I felt like I was in a dark place, and I needed to take advantage of this time to get granular with my issues. So I began seeing a therapist. I started to look into my issues and insecurities and unpack where they were coming from and how I needed to approach them in a more productive way. Growing is uncomfortable, but I am so proud of how much I have grown through this process. I've been able to face some of my insecurities head-on and ask myself hard questions. I've changed for the better, and I am extremely proud that I continue to receive therapy on a weekly basis to keep pushing and helping myself.

Everyone's journey is unique to them, and many of us need help beyond the expertise of our best friend. If you are struggling mentally or physically, make an appointment with a professional today. Having a Sunshine Mind sometimes means having to find the light when things get dark. We are all about reaching out for help—there is no shame in that. While therapy and getting help from a professional is extremely important, a huge part of helping ourselves and experiencing healing comes from the Spirit. Help from a wise professional partnered with a touch from God in prayer and worship is the best way to help yourself. Think of a flower. It requires both the sun and water to grow and thrive, right? We require the same in a physical and spiritual sense. To live in a Sunshine Mindset, we make sure to check in with our sources of love and support—our advisors and our God—to maintain balance, motivation, and healing.

THE SUNSHINE MIND WAY TO . . . HELP YOURSELF

Therapy is not a luxury; it is accessible to anyone, no matter their budget or schedule. You can get therapy through school, government services, or even some apps. We encourage you to do your research and find a form of therapy and a type of therapist that best fits your needs. Ask people you trust for guidance. Asking for help doesn't mean you're weak; it means you're stronger than you know.

BE NURTURED BY NATURE

Ask the beasts, and they will teach you;
*   the birds of the heavens, and they will tell you;*
or the bushes of the earth, and they will teach you;
*   and the fish of the sea will declare to you.*
Who among all these does not know
*   that the hand of the LORD has done this?*
In his hand is the life of every living thing
*   and the breath of all mankind.*

—JOB 12:7–10 ESV

Tanya

I find a lot of healing in planting my feet on the actual earth. I was dealing with immense heartbreak when a friend of mine suggested I come with her to Lake Tahoe. I spent my mornings running along sparkling lake water and through beautiful pine trees while listening to One-Republic's "Feel Again" on repeat. I spent my days swimming, water skiing, and paddleboarding. When I was on the water feeling weightless and supported by nature, I was in total peace and stillness. The therapeutic benefits of God's creation are often overlooked; it can truly help bring healing and restoration.

When was the last time your feet hit the ground? I usually put my shoes on before heading out the door for work, keep them on all day, and then walk back into my house at the end of the day with my shoes still on. My bare feet rarely touch the earth, but when they do, I feel it in my soul. If you can't get away for a weekend to go to the mountains, spend time by water, or immerse yourself in nature, figure out a way to do it around your house. I wildly underestimated the healing powers nature had over my soul.

We drive the same roads and walk the same paths almost every day. It's easy to grow used to the sights we see from our backyard or on our route to work. Things become routine as we pass them day after day, and that's when we start taking them for granted. To maintain a sunny disposition, we believe it is essential to take in the natural beauty that surrounds us. Pause for a moment to notice the magic of the clouds and watch the incredible weightless shapes they take. Or focus on a butterfly fluttering by. Give some attention to the sun, radiating from sunrise to sunset and giving life to everything it touches. See the amazing touch of the Creator all around you.

THE SUNSHINE MIND WAY TO . . .
BE NURTURED BY NATURE

Take time today to be nurtured by nature. Choose an outdoor picnic over indoor dining. Plant your bare feet on the natural ground. Walk around on your lawn. Feel the grass between your toes. If you're lucky to live near a beach, sink your feet into the sand. Connecting with nature will ground you, bringing you a sense of calm and peace.

WORK OUT WELL

Do you not know that your body is a temple of the Holy Spirit within you, whom you have from God? You are not your own, for you were bought with a price. So glorify God in your body.

—1 CORINTHIANS 6:19-20 ESV

Raquelle

Being physically strong can make you feel powerful from within. I've always found working out challenging and would often start an exercise class but not finish it, or start a fitness routine but not follow through on it. When the pandemic hit and life slowed down, I got into the routine of going on long walks every day. After about a month of these long walks, I craved walking even more, and my walks became even longer. My body felt so great that I decided to try Pilates, and I found that to be a great workout for me. I now do Pilates a few times a week, but with the busyness of life in full swing again, I have moments when I would rather stay in bed than get up. But whenever I go to the workout class, I never regret it. I feel better physically and mentally, and because of this I am more clear-minded and able to live out God's purposes for me each day feeling both physically and mentally strong.

Our bodies and minds influence each other. How we stand or sit has much to say about where we are mentally and emotionally. Sit up a little taller and roll those shoulders back. How does that make you feel? Empowered. Strong. Ready to take on the day. Now slouch your shoulders and allow yourself to slump forward. Notice the difference in how you feel? Less powerful. Lazy. Unhealthy, even. How we treat our bodies affects our minds and moods. And treating our bodies well is not only for our own benefit. God wants us to use our bodies to glorify him and to have the strength and energy to help others. When we're feeling our best, everyone benefits.

THE SUNSHINE MIND WAY TO . . . WORK OUT WELL

Be intentional with your workout routine. If you're like us and working out has always been tough for you, start with something simple like walking for fifteen minutes each day. Or try a workout like Pilates, slow-flow yoga, or barre—something that isn't so intense. Set reminders for yourself—a note on your desktop, a sticky note in your planner, an alarm on your phone—to keep your frame and your mood upright.

Day 59

CATCH A VISION

The plans of the diligent lead surely to abundance.

—PROVERBS 21:5 ESV

Tanya

I am a vision board queen. I've been making vision boards at the top of each New Year for as long as I can remember. When the year is coming to a close, I spend a lot of time reflecting. Where have I been this year? What did I do? Where did I focus a lot of my energy? What did I accomplish? What has been pulling at my heart? Then in the first week of January, I take about a week to create a new vision board. During this time I pray and think hard about what goes on the board. I'll never forget one year when I put a Grammy Award on my vision board. To me, this symbolized the goal of working at or hosting the Grammys. It turned out that God had even bigger plans. He won me a People's Choice Award that year! Having new goals and dreams always keeps me in a positive, forward-thinking headspace. Because I believe that my destiny is in God's hands, my happiness is not tied to checking everything off my vision board. Rather, my vision board serves as a guiding light to keep me on track and focused. I keep it in a place where I will see it every day. And you better believe I've saved every vision board I've made. It's incredible to see the goals and aspirations God has put in my heart and to remember how he has fulfilled each of them in his own way. I put *"New York Times* Bestselling Author" on my 2018 vision board. Clearly God's plan for me was just a few years off (wink, wink).

Having goals gives us purpose and drive. It's important to check in on your goals regularly to keep yourself accountable and on track. While long-term goals are extremely important, short-term goals are what eventually get us to those long-term goals. For example, if you want to write a book, your long-time goal might be to one day have a full manuscript written. And that's awesome! But what can you do today to help get you there? Break your goal down into bite-size bits and decide what you will dedicate at least one hour to over the next few days. Often words like *diligent* (Proverbs 21:5) can feel restrictive. But really, everything written in the Bible is there to better our lives. If you stick with something and you're diligent with it, you will see results in abundance.

THE SUNSHINE MIND WAY TO . . . CATCH A VISION

If the idea of a vision board is overwhelming, let us break it down for you:

- What are your career goals? Think small and big.
- What personal goals do you have—a new hobby, a longtime dream, something you keep meaning to start?
- What are your health goals—physical or mental?
- What are your relationship goals?

Pick one word or phrase for the year. This will be the guiding light in all your decisions. Do you want more of something specific? Make that your word. For example, one year Tanya's word was *purpose*, and every decision she made had to go back to her greater purpose. Some other examples: level up, unstoppable, upright, balance.

EMBRACE CHANGE

Be strong and courageous. Do not be afraid or terrified because of them, for the Lord your God goes with you; he will never leave you nor forsake you.

—DEUTERONOMY 31:6

Raquelle

We constantly have to accept and adjust to change—plans change, schedules change, even people change. Recently a few of my friends have gotten into serious relationships. I've always said I love being single—and I do. I value my time. But now that my friends have these romantic relationships, we don't see each other as much as we used to. When we're younger, we don't necessarily think about what will happen when people get married and prioritize partners. If we don't embrace these changes as positive growth, it can feel like a loss rather than a restructure. Any time we feel loss, we wonder, "Am I losing my good friend?" Loss requires us to be strong, have perspective, and know God created nature and that nature is always changing. It's unavoidable and needs to be embraced. When I look back on all the changes in my life, whether it be changes in moves, jobs, friends, I see it all as part of God's divine plan and am grateful for every single change. With God as our anchor, we can embrace these changes with gratitude for what has been, resilience in the transition, and hope for what's ahead.

Many of us fear change. It is the fear of the unknown. It's why some people stay in jobs they hate and relationships that are toxic. They settle, even if life feels stagnant. Friendships go through seasons of change. It can be hard (on both sides) when people who are close are experiencing different seasons of life. Maybe one just had a baby and the other is still in her single and dating phase. It can be difficult to find common ground when you're in such different places in life. Even the strongest of friendships experience this at some point. The Sunshine way is to embrace the change and meet the challenge. Deuteronomy 31:6 is compelling when you realize God is with you every step of the way: "Do not be afraid or terrified . . . , for the LORD your God goes with you." If you are changing careers and taking a leap of faith, if you are untangling your life from a long relationship, if your friendships are evolving in different directions, if you are moving far away from your current home and will be starting all over with new friends and a new community—whatever the big change is in your life, look at it as an opportunity to improve in the places you've been complacent. Embrace it as being from God, and face the unknown with positivity and confidence.

THE SUNSHINE MIND WAY TO . . . EMBRACE CHANGE

We should welcome the opportunity for growth. Change is exciting! It allows us to improve ourselves, open new doors, learn new things, and hit the reset button. Rather than allow fear or worry to dominate your life, take some time to answer these two questions: What change are you facing? What is good about the change happening in your life?

Here's a Sunshine Mind prayer for embracing change:

Lord,

Thank you that you are with me during all the changes that come my way. I am grateful for all that has been, and I pray that you would help me accept [insert change that is hard right now]. I pray that you would give me peace and hope, knowing that all things are working together for your plan for my life. Amen.

Day 61

BE INDEPENDENT

Each one should test their own actions. Then they can take pride in themselves alone, without comparing themselves to someone else, for each one should carry their own load.

—GALATIANS 6:4-5

Tanya

When I met my current boyfriend, one of the things he said he was first attracted to was my independence—not my eyes, not my personality, but my independence. I was at a place in my life where I was fully independent. I'd focused on saving my money versus spending it, cultivating friendships I knew would last a lifetime, and building a community I was passionate about. It was my self-sufficiency that led me to find him, one who respects me as much as I respect him. I can't say I've had that in my previous relationships. There was always an imbalance. And I can only blame myself for that. I didn't see myself as an equal; I saw myself as less than. I thought the man deserved the ultimate say and more respect, as he was the head of the house. But after I spent years of managing myself and my household, let me tell you that Tanya now looks back at Tanya then, and it's not even the same girl. In a good way!

I t's a cliché, but it's true—you've gotta be fully good on your own before you can fully give yourself to someone else. It's important for us to handle our own business so we can be the best version of ourselves. When we are the best versions of ourselves and are confident in that independent person God created us to be, then we attract a partner who not only values and respects our independence but has the same values and respect for themselves. This truth applies not only to romantic partners but any relationship.

Go to a workout class alone.

Sit next to someone new in class.

Go early to a dinner reservation and spend an hour sitting alone at the bar.

Take a solo vacation (it doesn't need to be far or long; could be just a weekend away).

Go on a date with zero expectation of a future.

Work out in only a sports bra. (Don't overthink it.)

Make baked goods and bring them to your neighbors.

Go see a movie alone.

START THE DAY WITH SUNSHINE

*In the morning, LORD, you hear my voice;
in the morning I lay my requests before you
and wait expectantly.*

—PSALM 5:3

Tanya

For any of you who are early-morning workers, I'm right there with ya. Waking up before the sun can quite literally feel dark. I used to slap off my alarm, slither out of bed, crawl to the bathroom, and sluggishly get my days going. I always thought waking up slowly and peacefully would lead to a peaceful day, but this wasn't true for me. Now I jump-start my days: I jump out of bed, light a candle (if there is no light yet, I'll make my own), take a cold shower to jolt my body into high gear, and make my bed to start with a feeling of accomplishment (yes, I read that study about the gross dust mites that thrive if you make your bed first thing, but I've decided to turn a blind eye and simply wash my sheets more often). When I walk into any room, I greet everyone with a bright smile and cheerful hello. Don't forget to bring the light wherever you go!

How many of you ask yourselves this question every day: It's three o'clock already? When the workday begins, we tend to put our heads down for hours, then suddenly, it's dinnertime. Our days are so busy, which is why the mornings are precious. Establishing a healthy, positive morning routine creates an energy for the day that can make you unstoppable. We know, we know—no one wants to set their alarm earlier than they absolutely have to. But the benefits will outweigh the costs. We enjoy listening to worship music while we go about our morning routines. Playing worship music allows us to spend time with God before we get the day going. Start off slowly by setting your alarm just five minutes earlier than you normally do. Spend that five minutes reading your devotional, studying a Bible passage, or saying some affirmations aloud. If you create a morning routine rooted in worship, your mind, body, and soul will shift and your energy will increase.

THE SUNSHINE MIND WAY TO . . .
START THE DAY WITH SUNSHINE

Here's our favorite Sunshine Mind morning routine:

- Before you get out of bed, list what you're most grateful for.
- Turn on your favorite worship music.
- Take a refreshing cold shower.
- Make your bed.
- Water before coffee (we try for at least thirty ounces).
- Light a candle (bring that light in).
- Take your vitamins.
- Say your daily mantra out loud. (Every morning, when I wake up my dog Sunny, I tell her, "It's going to be a bright and sunny day.")

FORGIVE SOMEONE

Judge not, and you shall not be judged. Condemn not, and you shall not be condemned. Forgive, and you will be forgiven.

–LUKE 6:37 NKJV

Raquelle

What exactly is forgiveness? Maybe you've heard people say, "Forgive because Christ forgave us," or "Unforgiveness is like drinking poison and expecting the other person to die." You probably hear these phrases and think, "Yes, I want to forgive, but practically speaking, how do I do that?" Tanya and I both know that the only way to truly live the Sunshine Mind life is to forgive and let go. This is a journey I've had to dive deep into, and I think the first step to forgiving is acknowledging your hurt and your pain. Writing it all down or saying it out loud during prayer time can help you to acknowledge the hurtful things that have happened to you. Then, if you feel like the other person is open to hearing your heart, you can talk to them in a loving way about how you feel. Maybe there is room for an apology. But even if they don't offer an apology, you still have to do the work to forgive.

If the other person is not open to talking about it, or if it's something you don't feel like you can share with them, keep surrendering it just to God. Sometimes forgiveness may require a daily surrendering for a long, long time, or sometimes it could mean doing something kind for that person to cancel out the negative and give you peace of mind. But more than anything, you daily have to say, "I forgive them, I forgive them," and work on seeing that person who hurt you as human. It really works. It may not be easy, but in the end it will set you free.

Forgiveness is about releasing animosity. It's a choice, really—a conscious decision not to retaliate or revel in revengeful thoughts. Moving on from this toxic mindset is a form of self-care. You know when you're stewing over something someone did, fantasizing about how you would tell them off if you had the chance? We've probably all done it. It's only natural to get upset when someone hurts you. You can certainly get your feelings off your chest, but do so in a private, progressive way, like writing a letter you won't ever send or telling yourself in the mirror what you would say to this person if given the opportunity. But then move on because staying in this space is all-consuming and miserable—it only hurts you. Anger is heavy on your heart and unhealthy for your spirit. You don't need to carry this around! In the Lord's Prayer we pray, "Forgive us our debts as we forgive our debtors." For us to live in the light, we have to release our emotional ties to the negative thoughts or feelings, and we need to forgive.

THE SUNSHINE MIND WAY TO . . . FORGIVE SOMEONE

Communicating your feelings is key to forgiving someone. And being open and honest about why you were hurt is important. But once you decide to forgive, you can't throw what they did to hurt you back in their face. Forgiveness doesn't mean saying, "I forgive you" and continuing to hold transgressions over someone's head. True forgiveness means moving forward and not looking back.

Here's a prayer that might be helpful:

Dear Lord,
Hold my hand as I navigate this pain. Open my heart to true forgiveness, and help me let go of any negative feelings I have. Allow me to forgive wholeheartedly and move forward with a clean slate and an open heart. Help me to speak kindly and extend your grace. Amen.

Day 64

PRACTICE SELF-CONTROL

*Like a city whose walls are broken through
is a person who lacks self-control.*

—PROVERBS 25:28

Raquelle

It's important to balance what we put into our bodies. It can initially feel good to consume large amounts of sugar or caffeine, but the aftereffect is never good. For example, I love coffee. I'm obsessed with coffee. I look forward to my coffee every single morning. But if I have more than one cup (which I always want to because I love coffee), I get all jittery from the caffeine and don't even enjoy the second cup. It's a disaster. One cup of coffee a day is all I need, which is a great example of "everything in moderation." Sometimes consuming too much of a good thing becomes unhealthy, which is why it's important to practice self-control.

People don't like to be told what to do. It can be an instant killjoy, like when your parents used to give you a curfew. But rules like curfews can protect us. Without guidelines, boundaries, or laws, life would be a free-for-all. As we get older, self-control comes into play more and more. If we don't limit ourselves and hold ourselves accountable, there's no telling how that might affect our health, relationships, and overall well-being. When Proverbs 25:28 compares a wall that has been broken through to a person lacking self-control, it's saying they are no longer a solid foundation for themselves. The lack of structure gives the wall no purpose; it's no longer separating the rooms, and you can't even hang something on this wall. There's no substance to a broken wall the way there is no dependability in a person without boundaries.

THE SUNSHINE MIND WAY TO . . . PRACTICE SELF-CONTROL

Spend a little time thinking about anything that has gotten out of balance in your life. What do you need to cut back on?

Identify something you enjoy that you can reduce consumption of this week in order to indulge in moderation.

I could cut back on _____.

OPEN UP TO OTHERS

*As iron sharpens iron,
so one person sharpens another.*

–PROVERBS 27:17

Raquelle

My friendship with Ashley is the definition of an iron-sharpens-iron friendship. She is the person I call to process pretty much everything—the good stuff, the bad stuff, and everything in between. I am the same friend for her. This kind of friendship took years to build, and after almost ten years of friendship, I can say I have found a confidant who's both mutual and trustworthy. Through this friendship I have realized how important it is to have a safe space to process and be challenged. It helps ignite fresh perspective and allows me to navigate challenges in a healthy way.

We're meant to live in community with other people. But when times get hard, it can be tempting to isolate ourselves. It's important to open up and share how we're doing, even if it's with only one other person. Brené Brown said shame can't survive in secrecy. This is important to remember because most of the time when we feel bad about ourselves, it's our negative thoughts taking over the truth of how things actually are. When we choose to be vulnerable and open up to a friend, we give them room to encourage us and speak truth to us, helping us overcome those negative thoughts.

THE SUNSHINE MIND WAY TO . . .
OPEN UP TO OTHERS

Ways to know if someone is healthy to open up to:

- Look at their track record—do they have healthy, solid friends around them?
- Do others consider them trustworthy?
- Are they happy for you when good things happen?
- Are they supportive and there for you when bad things happen?

FRIENDSHIP: REASON, SEASON, OR LIFETIME

Do not be misled: "Bad company corrupts good character."

—1 CORINTHIANS 15:33

Tanya

At one point I had a friend I'd known since our teen years. Once I was out of college, my work hours were all over the place because of the nature of my job, and I had a serious boyfriend who (by my own choice) took up a lot of my time. My friend was making me feel terrible for not spending as much time with her as she would've liked. She wasn't happy about my success at work, and she wasn't supportive of my relationship. She was upset that I was no longer available to be her party wing-girl, a role that no longer suited me. I felt guilty even though some of the things were out of my control, like a 5:30 a.m. call time. Her negativity took away from the positive feelings I should have been experiencing given the great opportunities I was getting at work and having a boyfriend I adored. After months of arguing, my friend and I couldn't get on the same page. Ultimately, I had to walk away from that friendship. It was taking more effort than either of us was willing to give. When I look back, the way we went our separate ways was actually amicable. I've often found that people are in our lives for a reason, a season, or a lifetime. Sometimes friends grow in different directions, and that's okay. Handle these moments with grace, think before you speak, and approach the split from a place of love and respect. You will never regret taking the high road, especially when it comes to friendships.

You know when you have a rotten piece of fruit in the fruit bowl? If that rotten piece of fruit is next to a good piece of fruit, both will end up bad. Our lives can be like that too. The people around you impact your character more than you realize. Why do you think memes that say, "Stay close to anyone who feels like human sunshine" are constantly going around? You are the company you keep, but sometimes we turn a blind eye to toxic relationships in our lives. We have to remember that we can pray for people to heal or wish them well without being around their negativity. If you've never experienced a breakup with a friend, then bless up, because it is awkward and horrible, albeit sometimes necessary. Sometimes friends can be negative about your relationship because they are unhappy with their own. Or they're resentful that you've found a great partner, while they're still living the single life. Some might resent that you put so much time and energy into your career, because they are in an unfulfilling profession themselves. You shouldn't expect anyone to be perfect, but shielding yourself from toxic relationships is important. Bad company corrupts good character.

THE SUNSHINE MIND WAY TO . . . CHOOSE GOOD FRIENDS

Take a hard look at the five people closest to you—the people with whom you spend your weekends, your happy hours, your birthdays. If someone in that circle constantly makes you feel anxious, pressured, or unhappy, it is time to reevaluate this relationship and see whether you can get it back on track or if you need to eliminate it from your life.

STOP PROCRASTINATING

Whoever watches the wind will not plant;
whoever looks at the clouds will not reap.

—ECCLESIASTES 11:4

Raquelle

I am the ultimate procrastinator. I work best under pressure, but sometimes procrastination is not the right move, as it can leave me feeling stressed and overwhelmed. When I have a lot to get done and don't want to leave it all to the last minute, I make a list on my phone of everything I need to do. When I do this, I try not to let the day go by without making sure I check everything off. If I'm struggling to complete the list, I hype myself up by putting on motivating music, doing a quick workout, or calling a friend to give me a boost. But, no—wait. That is the very definition of procrastination! Whoops. That's the behavior that causes me to fall off the tracks. It's okay to take a quick break, but make sure you get back to work right away.

Stop thinking and start doing. It's so easy just to talk about the things you want in your life—maybe it's a new project or adventure you've been planning for a long time. But you can't just will something into your life. You've got to get up and get going! Put your plan into action. God has given you these ideas and dreams for a reason, so when you put things off, you miss out on the fruit of doing something God has asked you to do. Take the first step today; show us what you're made of! We know you can do it.

THE SUNSHINE MIND WAY TO . . . STOP PROCRASTINATING

Make a list of things you've been procrastinating, putting them in order of urgency. Then write a date or a time next to each item and hold yourself accountable to getting each task done by its deadline. Be realistic with your expectations. If you need to schedule breaks in between, go ahead. But quickly find your way back to what takes priority.

FiND CONTENTMENT

*I have learned to be content
whatever the circumstances.*

–PHILIPPIANS 4:11

Raquelle

When I was filming season four of *Selena + Chef*, the house we were filming at in Malibu had no phone service except for Wi-Fi. I spend much of
my days on calls, so this was a big change for me. I soon found myself
using my phone a lot less due to the lack of service and quickly felt less
attachment to it. Don't get me wrong—I still checked my texts and social
media, but I felt like I could detach a bit and take breaks because there
was no cell service. It was a refreshing month for me, and it made me
realize the importance of taking breaks from my phone. That month also
gave me special memories with friends, and not having as much online
access allowed me to be more fully present. Because it was such a fulfilling time, I have tried since then to be less attached to my phone and
have become more content, not feeling like I have to answer every text,
call, or email immediately.

The book of Philippians, written by the apostle Paul, has a lot to say about contentment. In it, Paul says, "I know what it is to be in need, and I know what it is to have plenty. I have learned the secret of being content in any and every situation" (Philippians 4:12). I believe what Paul is saying here is that we have the power to be content in any and all circumstances. We have many apps and devices that can entertain us, but they can also breed discontentment. We feel content spending a relaxing night at home . . . until we scroll to see someone doing something extravagant and we think, "Oh, I wish I could swap places with them." This type of discontentment is dangerous to our minds and spirits. That's why it's important to unplug, enjoy life exactly as it is, and be content with our many blessings.

THE SUNSHINE MIND WAY TO . . . FIND CONTENTMENT

Many social media accounts out there make us feel like we're not enough, not successful enough, not exciting enough, not pretty enough. If you find yourself feeling less than when you scroll past someone's post, you have our permission to unfollow or hide that handle. Then turn off your phone and start enjoying the real world!

CHALLENGE YOUR PERSPECTIVE

Blessed are those who find wisdom,
those who gain understanding.

–PROVERBS 3:13

Raquelle

"The more that you read, the more things you will know. The more that you learn, the more places you'll go."⁴ I've always loved this quote by Dr. Seuss. When I'm stuck in a rut, reading opens my mind to worlds completely different from my own. As my perspective is broadened, I am able to connect with a greater variety of people and better understand other ways of living. This openness has allowed me to become friends with and work well with many types of individuals. Reading is a journey to wisdom, and as Proverbs 3:13 says, in return we gain understanding. Understanding helps us eliminate judgment and criticism and opens the door to knowledge and personal growth.

To us, knowledge and empathy go hand in hand. To be wise means to gain knowledge, and to understand is to have acceptance. As we learn more about other people and their lives and backgrounds and stories, we more fully understand them. The more knowledge we have, the better we understand and the wiser we become. Even in our relationship with God, the more time we spend with him, the more we understand his ways and are able to grow in our faith. Knowledge challenges our perspective and gives us the gift of understanding.

To challenge your perspective and help you grow in knowledge, find a new book outside the genre you typically read. Go into it with an open mind and prepare to learn!

If you typically read _____, pick up a title in _____— and vice versa.

Self-Help—Autobiography
Science Fiction—Young Adult
Nonfiction—Fantasy
Romance—Mystery

Day 70

PUT AWAY PRIDE

*Pride goes before destruction,
a haughty spirit before a fall.*

—PROVERBS 16:18

*First pride, then the crash—
the bigger the ego, the harder the fall.*

—PROVERBS 16:18 MSG

Raquelle

Former US secretary of state Condoleezza Rice gave a great example of living free from ego in an interview she did with Oprah. Condoleezza said she'll never forget the moment she was about to board Air Force One. It was then that she realized her life dream had come true. There she was with her dream job, stepping onto the president's airplane. The emotion she felt? Humility, not pride. She remembered thinking, "You should never assume it was just through your own smarts than everybody else that you got there. There are so many people who are as good as you were, who never quite made it to that place. And I try very hard to remember that I've been good, but I've been lucky and fortunate and blessed, too."[5] This story is a reminder that when good things happen to us, even if it took hard work to get there, these moments should humble us as opposed to giving us an ego. Often these blessings are God's favor, which doesn't make you better than anyone else. That's a lesson to remember for life. Be proud of your accomplishments, but don't let them give you an inflated sense of self. Instead, let them humble you and fill you with gratitude.

iving the Sunshine Mind life means living free from ego. When you have a real revelation of just how big God is and think about how he alone created all of us and everything in the world, it automatically eliminates the ego because the truth is, we are all human. No one is God, and no one person is better than another. We all eat. We all sleep. As the saying goes, we all put on our pants one leg at a time. Any of us could have been born into any circumstance, but God put you in yours and me in mine. Live with gratitude and humility, and put away pride.

THE SUNSHINE MIND WAY TO ... PUT AWAY PRIDE

Write down an accomplishment (or a whole list of accomplishments) you are proud of. Then give the accomplishment to God. Thank him for what he has done in your life. Let your heart fill with gratitude as you meditate on God's greatness. Gratitude eliminates the ego and puts the focus where it belongs.

TRY SOMETHING NEW

I am about to do something new.
See, I have already begun! Do you not see it?
I will make a pathway through the wilderness.
I will create rivers in the dry wasteland.

−ISAIAH 43:19 NLT

Raquelle

A friend recently shared a story with me about how being open to a new perspective helped her to find romantic love. In 2020 my friend found herself in a place where she felt like she needed to explore her thoughts and feelings on finding a love match because what she'd been doing wasn't working. She was feeling down about her life and starting to believe she would never find someone she could build a life with. What she discovered was that her fantasy of what she thought she wanted was unrealistic. She had been out of touch with what she actually wanted. My friend had chosen relationships based on what others thought would be best for her or who she thought seemed like a "cool" guy. After acknowledging her own feelings, she became hyperaware of what she was looking for and started to look forward, not back. As she focused more on the steps she needed to take to attract a healthy relationship, she used a dating app for the first time. There, after her first date, she found her match! Even with how well their dating was going, she still felt hesitant at first because she continued to hold on to the old version of what she thought she wanted. Eventually she was able to fully let go of her unrealistic expectations, and now she is in a healthy, beautiful relationship with someone who adores her. Trying something new—and changing her perspective—changed her entire life!

When was the last time you tried something new? A hobby you've always been drawn to? An adventure you've always wanted to try? What about a new behavior pattern? Or a new method for making decisions? Changing your perspective can help new experiences come alive for you, teach you new things, and result in tremendous personal growth. New experiences with others can spark a new you. When you change your thinking and your habits, you can become a better version of yourself. The new wings that you grow through the power of faith and the security of God's love will take you places you've never imagined.

THE SUNSHINE MIND WAY TO . . . TRY SOMETHING NEW

What is something you've been wanting to try? What fears or concerns are holding you back? Identify what's holding you back, and then push past the fear. What's waiting for you on the other side is so worth it! Make a list of new things to try, then start checking them off!

LOVE WiTHOUT ATTACHMENT

There is no fear in love; but perfect love casts out fear.

–1 JOHN 4:18 NKJV

Raquelle

As Dr. Maya Angelou said, "Love liberates. It doesn't just hold—that's ego."[6] When we love someone or something, it's only natural that we want to hold on to it. But real love releases. If someone I love has to move away to a different city, I won't be happy about it. I will miss them, and that makes me sad. I would much rather have this person close by; but if I love freely, I will want what is best for them. So when a new job takes my favorite neighbor to another state? Or a relationship moves my best friend across the country? It's okay for me to be sad, but I also need to say, "I'm happy for you. I want what's best for you. I choose to be happy for you."

oving without attachment—wow! Is that even possible? It's such a difficult thing to do because when we love someone, we naturally want to hold on to them. Why do we feel this way? Because we fear losing them. We fear we're not good enough. We fear change. We fear things will never be the same between us. We fear a lot of things. Love is the most vulnerable emotion, but it's important to be able to love without attachment because anything we hold on to—including people—can become an idol. God reminds us that perfect love casts out fear. Release your fear, and love without attachment.

THE SUNSHINE MIND WAY TO . . . LOVE WITHOUT ATTACHMENT

Think of someone you love a lot. Is fear causing you to hold on to anything in that relationship in an unhealthy way? If so, read this prayer aloud:

Dear God,
I thank you for [say their name]. I thank you for the gift of being able to love them so much. Now I surrender them to you. I want to be okay with [say the hard thing you've been holding on to] and to be able to love them freely, knowing that true love wants what's best for the other person. Thank you for giving me the strength to love without attachment. Amen.

CELEBRATE THE SUCCESS OF OTHERS

Let us consider one another in order to stir up love and good works, not forsaking the assembling of ourselves together, as is the manner of some, but exhorting one another, and so much the more as you see the Day approaching.

—HEBREWS 10:24-25 NKJV

Tanya

I will never forget the support and encouragement I received from the three women of the LADYGANG empire. *LadyGang* is a podcast hosted by Keltie Knight (she prefers to be first—love you, Keltie), Becca Tobin, and Jac Vanek. They have turned their podcast into a TV show, a tour, a book—they are basically building an empire. One could look at their female-led podcast as being in direct competition with my female-led podcast. Heck, in 2018 I was even up against them for the People's Choice Award for pop podcast of the year. But these girls are supporters all the way; they have gone out of their way to support and encourage me through every step of my journey. After I'd been on their podcast, Keltie called me to let me know that my episode was one of their most listened-to podcasts that year. I couldn't believe it. Me? Little ol' nothing, no-name Tanya Rad had more listens than some of the big-name celebs they'd had on their show? That info is not public knowledge, and Keltie didn't need to share it with me. But I'll never forget what she said during that phone call: "I don't want you to question how valuable you are." Keltie knew I struggled with imposter syndrome, and she wanted to encourage me to keep pushing forward. Her words meant a lot to me, and she continues to show me the importance of and value in celebrating each other's successes. That one little phone call made a huge impact on my life.

Celebrating the success of others is important. Being envious or jealous when good things happen to someone else is a toxic way to live. When you celebrate another person's success, you live a life that is happy and free. As Christians, we have an obligation to fellowship. God calls on us to exhort one another—to encourage each other. Our cultural norm is to do the opposite, especially when it comes to social media. We spew words of anger and hate, we lose empathy and compassion, we feel rage and animosity. This isn't the way God intended us to act toward each other. He wants us to love, encourage, and celebrate one another.

THE SUNSHINE MIND WAY TO . . . CELEBRATE THE SUCCESS OF OTHERS

Don't underestimate what an encouraging phone call or text can do for someone. If you feel like sending a message, send it! If you want to make a call, make it! Do it today. Be that light. Bring the sunshine to someone today—even to someone who would least expect it from you.

Day 74

REDiRECT YOUR WORRY

Can any one of you by worrying
add a single hour to your life?

—MATTHEW 6:27

Tanya

To hit the "refresh" button on my brain, I often hop in the shower, lather up, and watch my worries wash away down the drain. When I step out of the shower, I'm literally clean and fresh, and I tell myself that everything that had been negatively affecting me is no longer part of who I am. This practice came into play as I awaited results from my doctor a few years ago. I received a call that something came back abnormal and had to go back for additional testing. This news sent me into a tailspin. What if it's this? Or worse, what if it's that? I had zero details, yet here I was worrying before I even knew what to be worried about. When the second results came back letting me know there was nothing serious to worry about, I truly discovered that worrying doesn't change the outcome—it only takes away from your present joy. The week I spent planning for the absolute worst, I could have been full of light and laughter, but instead I let my mind go wild with worry.

on't borrow tomorrow's problems. Cross that bridge when you get to it. These are just a few of the lines we hear from others when we worry aloud. But this advice is easier said than done. We love to tell ourselves stories about things that haven't yet happened—if they will at all. The what-ifs of the world are enough to drive us insane. When you catch yourself ruminating your way into a tizzy, it's time to redirect. Redirecting is different from distracting. To distract is to play games or tricks, and that isn't what the Sunshine Mind is about. Rather, stop the unproductive self-talk by moving on to something else and washing your worries down the drain.

THE SUNSHINE MIND WAY TO . . . REDIRECT YOUR WORRY

Do you feel yourself getting caught up in a world of worry? Redirect your thoughts by keeping your heart and your mind busy:

- Put together a puzzle.
- Paint your nails.
- Clean your house from top to bottom.
- Listen to an upbeat playlist.
- Help somebody else with a problem they're having.
- Take that shower!

CONFRONT YOUR WEAKNESSES

He said to me, "My grace is sufficient for you, for my power is made perfect in weakness." Therefore I will boast all the more gladly about my weaknesses, so that Christ's power may rest on me.

—2 CORINTHIANS 12:9

Tanya

I don't love making decisions. I can organize. I can clean. I'm able to handle a to-do list like nobody else. But when it comes to making decisions, I collapse under the pressure. Decisions as basic as what food to order or what movie to watch? Not for me. Don't even get me started on coming up with the title for this book. That was a tough process for me. My weakness in making decisions can be problematic in certain areas of my life, but, as with all my other weaknesses, I've found it helpful if I can talk through my decision-making dilemma with my partner, my coworkers, and my friends. That way they can understand me, support me, and even help me overcome my weakness. Instead of keeping my weaknesses hidden and trying to deal with them (or not deal with them) on my own, I always prefer to have the loving support of others.

God's grace is not only for forgiveness for the things we've done, it's for our weaknesses too. Second Corinthians 12:9 says that when we recognize our weaknesses, we should boast about them, not feel shame about them. God will fill us with his power and grace so that we lack nothing. We are all saved by grace, so it's perfectly natural and okay to have flaws. While all of us have weaknesses, often we feel a need to conceal our weak areas. We hide them because we feel ashamed of them. But speaking about these weaknesses—out loud, to others—can break their power over us. When they're no longer hidden, they don't seem as scary or shameful or embarrassing, and the people who love us can better understand us and help us.

THE SUNSHINE MIND WAY TO . . . CONFRONT YOUR WEAKNESSES

Make a list of your biggest weaknesses. Next to each one, write down a way you can ask for help from others.

For example:

TANYA'S LIST

DECISION MAKING. I'll give two options and let someone else make the final call.

SAYING YES TOO MUCH. I'll include people in my plans so I'm not spreading myself too thin or flaking on commitments.

PRIORITIZING MYSELF. I'll start communicating my needs and plans to my partner.

FIND PEACE IN BEING ALONE

Even though I walk
through the darkest valley,
I will fear no evil,
for you are with me;
your rod and your staff,
they comfort me.

—PSALM 23:4

Tanya

When I had an MRI for the first time, the doctor told me I had to go into the spaceship-looking tube *alone*. No one in the room with me. No one to talk to so I could be distracted. Nope, alone. Sans. Solo. So you know what I did after I was strapped into place and sent on my merry way into the silver tube abyss? I talked to God. I prayed for stillness. I prayed for the people in my life. I prayed because I knew God was there with me, for he is with me always. We are never truly alone because God is always with us. Now, we don't need to set a place for him at the table (unlike what I did when I was manifesting my life partner, but that's a different story for a different day). But it's good to remember that God is with us, always. If you're ever in a situation where you are approaching a journey or an event alone, don't let that fear bog you down. You are never alone. God is with you.

Being alone is something many of us fear. The word *alone* itself can create anxiety. Why are we so afraid of being alone? We can do great things alone! Ride a bike. Rollerblade. Play solitaire. Do a craft. Watch whatever TV show we want. Read. Write. The list goes on! During my many years of singledom, I (Tanya here) received a lot of messages that expressed confusion, with the general consensus of, "How do you seem so happy alone?" This question I could answer with great ease and joy because I was able to talk about the love of Jesus in my life. I know with certainty that God is with me every step of the way. Even when I'm walking through the darkest valley, he's with me. So, to me, the words *single* and *alone* were not one and the same. Single meant unattached. Single meant freedom with my time. Single meant possibilities. Single didn't mean alone because I know I'm never alone—God's with me.

THE SUNSHINE MIND WAY TO . . .
FIND PEACE IN BEING ALONE

When the fear of being alone creeps in, make a list of the people who love and support you, and reach out to them! When you share how you are feeling, you can receive exactly what you need—a hand, a prayer, or knowledge that someone is there.

Also, being alone can be a blessing. This is when you can be your truest self and hear your inner voice most clearly. This is the time to make plans, set goals, and push yourself to grow. Rolling solo has many perks. You can learn a new instrument, listen to the music you like, write a song, or write a book without interruption. When it comes to feeling a little lonely, we find it's best to avoid social media because it has a way of making us feel alone in the bad way. Instead, cook something challenging, go into crazy organization mode, or find a workout on YouTube that you can do from your living room. Lean into the positives and know there are countless people who would love to swap places with you!

LOVE EVERYONE GOD'S WAY

Love one another. As I have loved you, so you must love one another.

–JOHN 13:34

Raquelle

I try to approach every relationship, whether it be with family, friends, or a romantic partner, with the knowledge that I can't change someone. I know when I haven't been acting as the best version of myself, a friend trying to change me never works; it only makes me not want to open up to them. I can ask for advice or hear out a friend who I know has my best interest at heart, and I think it's important to welcome opinions from people we love and trust, but ultimately, someone loving me unconditionally through the ups and downs is what helps most. Through those experiences, I've realized that the only way to have healthy relationships is to accept people as they are. And when I love and accept someone, they rise to be the best versions of themselves.

With the people we love and care about, we often project our own expectations onto them. But it isn't fair to pin our own hopes and desires on others, expecting them to want what we want. God created each of us uniquely, and he loves us for who we are as individuals. Because of this, we need to love and accept each exactly as we are.

It's important to accept people for who they are—nothing more, nothing less. This doesn't mean you don't give advice when people ask for it or that you don't challenge your friends when they need it, but you do have to accept people as they are. Oprah did a great interview with Dr. Shefali on letting go of expectations. Oprah talked about how one of the girls she supports by paying for her schooling and other needs was having a hard time at college. Oprah said she realized she, as the girl's mother figure, had talked the girl into attending this particular school because she had put her own hopes and dreams on the girl. When Oprah was that age, she wanted nothing more than to go to that college and couldn't, so she thought, "Who wouldn't want that opportunity?" Oprah thought she only wanted the best for this girl, but beneath her wanting the best were the chains of expectation. Oprah said she now comes at the situation from a different perspective: She realizes she can open doors for the girl, but she gives the girl freedom to choose the way she wants to go—or not go at all. When you accept others for who they are, you take the stress off them—and off yourself.

THE SUNSHINE MIND WAY TO ...
LOVE EVERYONE GOD'S WAY

If you're struggling to love and accept others as God loves and accepts them, say this prayer:

Dear God,
Help me to love the people in my life the way you love me. Help me to let go of my expectations, knowing that you satisfy all my deepest needs. Help me to be able to love others from a place of abundance, accepting people exactly as they are. Amen.

KNOW GOD'S LOVE

Long before he laid down earth's foundations, he had us in mind, had settled on us as the focus of his love, to be made whole and holy by his love.

—EPHESIANS 1:4 MSG

Raquelle

I remember my grandpa Mike telling me a story about his first encounter with God, a story he also writes about in his amazing book, *70 Golden Threads of Grace* by Mike Stevens. He was twelve years old and was attending a small church in the countryside of North Wales when he first heard the words of the famous hymn: "Turn your eyes upon Jesus, look full in his wonderful face. And the things of earth will grow strangely dim in the light of his glory and grace."[7] Grandpa Mike said that at the time he heard the song, he couldn't fully identify what he experienced, but he knew something had touched his heart. In later years, after he had been taught the foundations of faith and learned about the presence of God, he came to recognize that in hearing the words of the hymn, he became consciously aware of God. He said he now looks back on that time in awe of God's predestined choosing of him. At nearly eighty years old, he still gets teary-eyed over this experience. It reminds him that everything in his life has been a result of God's gracious love. We all have much to learn from those who have lived longer than we have, and the fact that an experience my grandpa had when he was only twelve years old can still bring tears to his eyes reminds me of how special we are to God.

No matter what age we are or who we are, God created us to live out our own individual lives. He created us and he loves us, which we can forever be in awe of. Even before God created the earth, he had us specifically in mind. This is something our human minds can hardly comprehend. God loves us so much and chose us to be here on earth specifically at this time. Take a moment to let that soak in: before the creation of the earth, God had you on his mind, and he chose you. If you're ever having a blah day, remember this and it will remind you of the importance of your life. Know that God loves you and chose you for this time for a very special reason.

THE SUNSHINE MIND WAY TO . . . KNOW GOD'S LOVE

Feeling down today? Feeling unloved? Pray this prayer to remind you of who you are and who created and loves you:

Dear God,
Thank you for creating me and choosing me for this specific time on earth. I'm so amazed! Please help me to continue to experience your love and presence in powerful ways. I pray that others will experience your love and presence too. Amen.

STOP THE GOSSIP

A perverse person stirs up conflict,
and a gossip separates close friends.

—PROVERBS 16:28

Raquelle

I work in the entertainment industry, which because of its superficial nature, can be filled with a lot of insecure people. When people feel insecure, they tend to gossip because they believe that putting someone else down can make them feel bigger themselves. But it does just the opposite. It only creates more shame, unhappiness, and insecurity. I don't know one person who hasn't been guilty of engaging in gossip from time to time (myself included), but the aftereffect is never, ever good. Trying to live the Sunshine Mind way, I aim to talk about other people in a way they would approve of, and I always try to respect the trust that others have given me.

et's be honest—gossip is a part of life. To varying degrees, we all partake in it. But we must keep ourselves in check, as gossip can ruin relationships. Think about your closest friends and how much you love them. Now think about the power of words. Remember the personal thing a friend told you and not anyone else? Someone was willing to be vulnerable with you, and having someone feel safe with you is a great privilege, so think about that the next time you're tempted to spread something someone told you in confidence. You might get attention from spreading it, but you also might lose a friend. Think about what Proverbs 16:28 says: your sharing that personal information could destroy trust with someone and end your friendship. And trust and friendship are two of the most special things someone can give you. Respect your relationships, and resist the urge to gossip.

THE SUNSHINE MIND WAY TO . . . STOP THE GOSSIP

Next time you're tempted to gossip, stop yourself. Instead share something positive about that person. Below is a helpful guide on how we would steer the conversation.

1. **GOSSIP:** "Did you hear about Javon and Kayla's relationship?"
   RESPONSE: "You know what? I did hear about it, and I wish them well. That must be really hard what they're going through."
2. **GOSSIP:** "Did you hear about Joe and Sabrina's money troubles?"
   RESPONSE: "Who hasn't had trouble with money at some point? I remember this one time . . . (personal story)."
3. **GOSSIP:** "Did you hear Jenny and Rosie are fighting?"
   RESPONSE: "It's sad when two friends fight. I hope they find their way out of it soon."

STOP TAKiNG YOURSELF So SERiOUSLY

One's pride will bring him low,
but he who is lowly in spirit will obtain honor.

—PROVERBS 29:23 ESV

Tanya

I will never forget the time I shared my fart story on my podcast. Is the story embarrassing? Beyond. Could I have left it where it happened and never shared it publicly? For sure. But I don't take myself that seriously, and you know what? Everybody farts! I'm over the narrative that if we are ladies, we don't burp or fart or do naughty things. Nope, not true. It happens to all of us. When I shared this embarrassing story of farting out loud in a nail salon, it literally moved Becca from laughter to tears, and I was overwhelmed by the positive response from our listeners. Yes, we all obsess over carefully curated content on social media and strive to maintain the perception that our lives are perfect, but in reality a lot of life is happening between all those posts. I don't care about hiding the embarrassing moments of my life because I am human, and that is okay. Next time you see your pride getting in the way of any situation, just remember the nail salon fart story and don't take yourself so seriously. If you'd like to hear the play-by-play of this glorious adventure, check out episode 30, "Breaking Wind and Breaking Away," of *Scrubbing In with Becca Tilley & Tanya Rad*, specifically from 18:55 to 22:06, and have a good laugh on me.[8]

The Bible talks a lot about pride. The problem with pride is that when you're prideful, you have an unhealthy presumption of superiority. Raquelle here, and I love this quote from Andrew Murray: "Pride must die in you, or nothing of Heaven can live in you."[9] Pride corrupts the soul. When I think back on things I've said or done that I'm not proud of, most of them came from a place of pride, and I've regretted what I said or did every single time. We have to counterbalance pride with humility and not take ourselves too seriously. We also allow pride to stop us from doing a lot of things in life. You can be too prideful to go on a dating app, even though you are seeking a life partner your heart so deeply desires. You can be too prideful about possibly feeling out of place at your first workout class, even though you desperately want to start living a more active lifestyle. You can be too prideful to feel like an outsider at an event, so you stay home and watch TV every night even though you've been longing to find community. You can be too prideful to admit you were wrong or to try to understand someone else's perspective, so you waste precious hours or days being in a fight or staying angry, losing moments when you could connect with someone. Stop taking yourself so seriously. Lose the pride, focus on others, and start living a better—and more fun—life.

THE SUNSHINE MIND WAY TO . . . STOP TAKING YOURSELF SO SERIOUSLY

When we take ourselves too seriously, we cast a dark cloud over what should be fun and joyful. Life isn't perfect and neither are we. Thank God for that! How boring would life be if everything went according to plan? We're going to stumble, slip, and fall. We will miss a flight, flunk a test, slip on a banana peel. Of *course* I would leave the self-tanner on too long and look like an Oompa

Loompa the day before my best friend's wedding. But rather than skip out on what will be an awesome occasion, I'd chose to be in on the laughter and sing about the golden ticket all night long. God doesn't want us walking through life in tears, so we might as well laugh.

If you take yourself too seriously, try these tips:

ASK YOURSELF. Will this matter five years from now? Or even five days?

MAKE AN EFFORT TO LAUGH MORE. Don't watch too many *Dateline* episodes in a row. Be sure to check in on *Friends*, *Modern Family*, and other light-hearted comedies that show people slipping up often—and laughing about it.

FOCUS ON THE GOOD. If your flight was delayed, see if the airport has a good restaurant or store.

LEARN TO JOKE ABOUT YOUR SHORTCOMINGS. If you're superclumsy, always dropping or spilling things, add a "ta-da!" every time you pull a "you."

REACH OUT TO SOMEONE

We urge you, brothers and sisters, warn those who are idle and disruptive, encourage the disheartened, help the weak, be patient with everyone.

–1 THESSALONIANS 5:14

Tanya

Ten years ago I was in a season of life in which I was a shell of my former self. I had just gone through a breakup that had changed the course of my life. I didn't know who I was as a woman. I didn't know what I wanted to do, where I wanted to live, who my friends were. I was lost. I wasn't sleeping well. I cried constantly. I was a mess. My offices were down the hall from E! at the time, and I often saw Jason Kennedy in the small kitchen when I was heating up coffee or grabbing a snack. Jason and I weren't yet friends beyond our casual run-ins in the kitchen or hallways. During this time, I had started to use the hallways as a place to collect myself when I didn't want to cry in my office. And Jason noticed that I, the hallway girl, wasn't well. My eyes were visibly puffy from all the tears. Jason didn't owe me anything—we were basically strangers. He could have turned a blind eye and gone about his day. Instead, he chose to talk to me and invite me to his Bible study. He didn't ask me a single question about why I was upset; he simply extended his hand to me. At that point, I'd tried everything else. I'd gone through my drinking phase, my partying phase, my movies-and-ice-cream phase, but nothing worked. So I said yes to the Bible study, and I'm so glad I did. There, I was greeted with smiles and hugs and a discussion that was so relatable and relevant to my life. I felt like I was surrounded by like-minded people who were filled with hope and happiness. That night turned my life around, and I'll never be able to thank Jason enough for what he did. At that Bible study I also met Raquelle, one of my best friends (and, of course, the coauthor of this book). I finally found something that felt right, and that is where my relationship with God and my journey as a Christian truly began.

First Thessalonians 5:14 reminds us that ministry is not entirely up to spiritual leaders. We are all called to cheer up the disheartened, not give up on the idle, and encourage those who feel weak. Go out of your way today to extend a hand to someone outside your circle. Find someone who looks like they need a friend, and invite them to your weekly game night or Bible study or to grab a quick cup of coffee. You never know how big of an impact a small gesture can make on someone's life.

THE SUNSHINE MIND WAY TO . . . REACH OUT TO SOMEONE

My boyfriend and I started hosting Taco Tuesdays with this exact intention—reaching out to people. The two of us are social and outgoing but realize that many people struggle with finding meaningful friendships and relationships. We wanted to create a space where all our friends feel welcome. It's a weekly gathering of food and drink and laughter and games, something consistent friends can count on. We invite couples, friends who don't know anyone else invited, neighbors, friends from social media, and anyone we feel a connection to. Our hope in creating this event is for people to know that even if everything feels like it's going wrong in their lives, they have a happy and safe space to be at least once a week.

I encourage you to create your own safe haven for others. It doesn't need to be as elaborate as our Taco Tuesdays (you know I sure love me a festive theme), but something weekly or bimonthly or even monthly can provide consistency, friendship, and a safe place for people in your life. Consistency is the key.

Here are some other ideas:

SUNDAY PiCNiCS AT THE PARK. Potluck picnic with a speaker afterward.

FRiDAY GAME NiGHTS. Play board games, card games, video games. Or maybe even get a group together to attend sporting events—whatever your heart desires.

BiBLE STUDY. I had a couple of women's Bible study groups that would meet at restaurants around town every other week. It was fun to get to know the girls and explore the restaurants in our city.

REALIZE YOUR HAPPINESS

Enjoy what you have rather than desiring what you don't have. Just dreaming about nice things is meaningless—like chasing the wind.

—ECCLESIASTES 6:9 NLT

Tanya

In the past, I've sometimes attached my happiness to something external. For me, it was always tied to my professional career. I always sought to land the gig, win the award, and sell out the tour, but let me tell you where that led me. I'd achieve a goal, then ask, "What's next?" How could I do more, reach the next goal post? I could never simply enjoy the moment. I attached my happiness to success, and I always wanted more. Some people attach their happiness to objects. That isn't me because I've never needed a flashy car or designer clothes, but when we attach happiness to anything—objects, success, popularity—we will never be fully satisfied. We constantly want the next hit or the next high or the next thing. It took me a long time to realize that my happiness is inside me. I carry it with me every day. When I realized that, my mentality changed. I realized that my happiness was mine and that no person or situation could take it away from me.

If you have unrealistic expectations for yourself, it's time for a reset. If you feel like you need a constant dose of accomplishments, praise, awards, success, or money to feel happy, it's time to reevaluate. Your happiness is yours. It's not tied to the way the world sees you. Desiring what you don't have is the surest way to feel miserable and miss out on the present. Living in LA, I (hi, it's me, Tanya) am at the epicenter of people striving for material success, and I can honestly say it doesn't make anyone any happier. I'm not saying that aspiring for more or wanting nice things is wrong, because it's not. And having dreams is important. But when we fixate on these, we miss out on what we have right now. The more we focus on gratitude for what God has given us, the more we create space for abundance in our lives.

THE SUNSHiNE MiND WAY TO . . .
REALIZE YOUR HAPPINESS

What makes you happy? Don't think of what friends, family, or society says should make you happy; think of your own personal feelings. Then write down what comes to mind.

- People who make me happy: _____
- Places that make me happy: _____
- Things that make me happy: _____
- Activities that make me happy: _____
- Memories that make me happy: _____

RECEIVE GRACEFULLY

Ask and it will be given to you; seek and you will find; knock and the door will be opened to you.

—MATTHEW 7:7

Raquelle

A few years ago, I realized that sometimes it can be hard for me to receive a compliment. I think this is because there is a vulnerability in receiving, the same way there is a vulnerability in asking. For example, if someone says, "I love your outfit—you look so nice today," if you don't believe that yourself or you have a hard time accepting it, you might say things like, "Oh, this thing? I just threw it together last minute, it's nothing" instead of just accepting and saying thank you. I know I've been there. Or when it comes to asking, I know that the more my responsibilities have grown, the more I've had to ask others for help with projects. I used to try to do everything on my own because I didn't want to burden anyone, but the truth is we need each other. How can a company expand if you don't ask for help and bring more people on board? This is something I've learned and continue to learn, but I have found so much blessing in learning to receive and to ask for help.

The Bible talks about the importance of "asking" in order to receive. We live in a culture that sometimes emphasizes the "girl boss" mentality of "I don't need anyone or anything." But the truth is, we need each other and we need help. You're no less of a girl boss if you need to lean on others. Think about how important it is for us to seek God and all that we receive from him when we do. It's an act of receiving that brings us so much peace. God has loved us and also equipped us to receive from others. Healthy, loving relationships are one of the greatest gifts God has given us, and he blessed us with them so that we not only give to others but also receive from them, the same way we receive from him.

THE SUNSHINE MIND WAY TO . . . RECEIVE GRACEFULLY

The next time you are tempted to "reject" a compliment or stop someone from treating you to something, instead of saying, "Oh, no, I don't look great tonight. I just got ready super quick," or, "Thanks, but I can buy my own coffee," practice receiving gracefully. Simply say thanks and then receive with gratitude. Your acceptance of the gift means a lot to the person on the other end, as being able to give is one of life's biggest blessings.

BE A BLESSING

*Don't forget to do good and to share
what you have because God is pleased
with these kinds of sacrifices.*

—HEBREWS 13:16 CEB

Tanya

Being a blessing doesn't necessarily have to be an act of service; sometimes being a blessing means being your true self. God created me to be a loud, outspoken, confident, unashamed, modern woman. I stomp to the beat of my own drum, and I'm open about everything—even topics that are taboo in many public forums. One topic I'm outspoken about is my period. Why is it that even though 51 percent of the population is women, we are still embarrassed to talk about our periods, carry tampons, or share our uncomfortable stories? I will never forget my struggle with chronic UTIs. I had tried everything, including changing laundry detergent and the style of underwear I wore (granny panties are my new BFF; ain't no shame in my game). And then one day a listener suggested I try pelvic floor physical therapy. How in my thirty years on this earth had I never heard of such a thing? Well, it ultimately ended up changing my chronic pain forever. I reached back out to that woman and said, "Thank you for being such a blessing!" One little message from a stranger was a major blessing in my life. And I want to be a blessing for others too. So I walk to the restaurant bathroom with my tampon held high, and I post all my uncomfortable stories on social media in hopes that they encourage other women to do what makes them happy and comfortable and not to feel ashamed. Be a blessing by sharing knowledge and by being yourself—someone will be glad you did.

ur calendars are filled with checklists, appointments, projects, work meetings, conference calls, kids' activities, vet appointments—you name it. But something we don't usually schedule into our days is taking time to help others. Helping others can easily become an afterthought or added to the "when I have time" column, but God calls us to do good and be a blessing to others. We're supposed to be a blessing not only to our close friends, family, and coworkers but also to those we don't spend a lot of time with. Schedule "doing good" into your calendar today, and be a blessing to others.

THE SUNSHiNE MiND WAY TO . . . BE A BLESSiNG

Sharing your sunshine and light anonymously can be a surprise blessing in someone's day. Here are a few ideas for how to put a smile on a stranger's face:

- Fill a row of parking meters with coins or swipe your card, especially if you see any that are running low on time. You might save someone from getting a ticket!
- Going a bunch of places today? Anonymously leave a trail of cash for people to find. (You can leave the cash in an envelope with a note, letting them know it's a gift.) Headed to a workout class? Leave it on the treadmill. Going to the store? Shove it between some boxes of rice. Popping into the office? Leave it by the coffeepot.
- Collect the stray shopping carts left all over the parking lot and put them back where they belong.
- Help an elderly person or a mom with little kids load groceries into their car.
- If you have a garden, pick some flowers and leave a bouquet on your neighbor's front doorstep. Don't have a garden? Pick up some flowers from the store instead.

Day 85

SPREAD THE SUNSHINE

This is my commandment: love each other just as I have loved you.

—JOHN 15:12 CEB

Raquelle

When I think of what it looks like to spread the sunshine, I immediately think of Tanya. I'm not sure I know anyone who does a better job of this in their day-to-day life. She pays attention to all the details, whether it's writing a note of encouragement for a coworker or her boyfriend to start their day or making goodie bags for her friends on pretty much every holiday. She helps women who reach out to her on Instagram to navigate challenges with their menstrual cycles or deal with breakups. She truly cares and spreads light to strangers, people close to her—you name it. She is a light to everyone. She doesn't miss a moment. I see her live out John 15:12 to the fullest every day, and her life is so fruitful because of it. I think we can all learn from her example.

The Sunshine Mind isn't only about living a bright and happy life for yourself, it's also about spreading the sunshine, sharing that light with others. We all go through seasons of life that bring their own peaks and valleys. If you are at a peak, great! But don't sit in that happiness alone—share it and spread it all around! Jesus loves us in an extraordinary and beautiful way. It's up to us to share that love and spread the sunshine to everyone around us.

THE SUNSHINE MIND WAY TO . . . SPREAD THE SUNSHINE

What do you normally get in the mail? Doctor bills? Gas bills? Jury duty notices? Coupons from Bed Bath & Beyond? (Actually, those BBB coupons make my day, so let's take those out of the mix.) Our mailboxes are usually inundated with junk and bills. Boring! Let's turn that around today. Pick five people who could use some light right now, and write a card to each of them. To help you get going, here are some of our favorite quotes for specific circumstances:

- For a friend going through heartbreak and needing *comfort*: "Sometimes good things fall apart so better things can fall together."
- For a sorority sister applying for a job and seeking *affirmation*: "Confidence is the most beautiful thing you can possess."
- For a family member dealing with health issues and needing *strength*: "Where there is no struggle, there is no strength."
- For a coworker burning the candle at both ends and struggling with *balance*: "The key is not to prioritize what's on your schedule but to schedule your priorities."
- For a new parent who's *overwhelmed*: "There is no such thing as a perfect parent. So just go be a real one."

CARE FOR CREATION

Do not pollute the land where you are. . . . Do not defile the land where you live and where I dwell, for I, the LORD, dwell among the Israelites.

—NUMBERS 35:33-34

Tanya

I met my professional mentor when I was nineteen years old. His name is Scot Finck, and he is someone I've admired in the entertainment industry because of his integrity and character. He has truly been a guardian angel sent from God. Upon our second meeting, I noticed one very special thing about Scot. Wherever we went, if there was trash lying around, he picked it up and threw it away. No trash can nearby? No problem. Scot would put the trash in his pocket and throw it away when he got back to the office. This act stuck with me. How many times did I walk by trash-infested areas and just look at them with disgust but not do a thing about it? I'll never forget Scot's response when I asked him why he picked up trash. "I'm a steward of the earth," he said. "If not us, who does she have to protect her?"

How often do you see an empty water bottle or candy wrapper on the ground and think to yourself, "Eew, who does that?" before continuing on your way. To be real, we usually do too. But why not take the next unnatural step and pick up the litter and discard it ourselves? Being the better person often means taking responsibility for someone else's failure to act. And acting to protect the earth is always the right thing to do. God created this beautiful earth for us to live on: the vibrant sunrises that start our days, the breathtaking sunsets that end our evenings, the endless sparkling oceans that captivate and calm us, the snowcapped mountains that bring serenity and peace, the beautiful flowers that bring us joy. He was meticulous in his creation, and our job is to go out of our way to care for it.

THE SUNSHINE MIND WAY TO . . . CARE FOR CREATION

Be like my friend Scot today. Be mindful of the trash in your path. If you see something lying on the ground, pick it up even if there isn't a trash can nearby. Want to go even bigger? Grab a giant trash bag and walk your neighborhood or a public park. Or look for organized community cleanups or beach cleanups happening in your area. As you care for creation, post on your social media feeds and encourage your friends to do the same. Don't forget to hashtag #SunshineMindBook.

PUT A SMILE ON YOUR FACE

A cheerful look brings joy to the heart;
good news makes for good health.

—PROVERBS 15:30 NLT

Tanya

I'll never forget the day I discovered the power of my own smile. I was in my workout class, running on the treadmill. It was toward the end of class, and I was burning out of energy. All we had to do was hold our sprint for thirty more seconds, but I didn't think I could do it any longer. My boyfriend came over and said, "If you feel like giving up, look in the mirror and smile. It will hold you through." And guess what? He was right! Now anytime I tire during my workout (or during life in general), I look at myself in the mirror and put a giant smile on my face.

We tend to overlook the value of a simple smile. In Proverbs 15:30, God reminds us that a cheerful look brings joy to the heart. We go about our lives with a baseline look of vacancy on our faces, which naturally happens as we're caught up in reflecting on how our day is going, everything we still have left to do, and what meetings or projects are coming up next. But Proverbs tells us that a smile can change our outlook and change our lives, that a cheerful countenance can bring us happiness and even good health. Never underestimate the power of putting a smile on your face!

THE SUNSHiNE MiND WAY TO . . .
PUT A SMiLE ON YOUR FACE

Did you know the act of smiling alone signals your brain to be happy? It's true! When you smile, your brain releases dopamine, endorphins, and serotonin. These neurotransmitters lower anxiety and give you a hit of happiness. Next time you catch yourself running around at baseline, switch it up to a smile. When you're working out, driving, doing the dishes, taking a shower, reading a book—give your best grin and see how much it elevates your vibe.

THRIVE IN YOUR CURRENT SEASON

There is a time for everything,
and a season for every activity under
the heavens.

—ECCLESIASTES 3:1

Tanya

This past awards season was the first time in years I wasn't asked to work the red carpet as a correspondent. I was crushed. As I sat on the sidelines watching it all unfold, my imposter syndrome came raging back at an all-time high. I wondered if I wasn't good enough for the job or maybe someone didn't like my personality. Shortly after I realized I wasn't getting called to work the red carpet, I got my puppy, Sunny. And boy, I had not anticipated the way this sweet little girl would change my life. She kept us up all night, and all day much of my focus was on when to feed her, where to walk her, and who was going to watch her when we had places to go and things to do. After a while, being a dog mom became more manageable, but when I think back on how much time and focus awards season requires of me, I realize I wouldn't have been able to balance my usual workload with the needs of my sweet Sunny girl. There is a time for everything, and this was my season to become a dog mama. And this sweet girl has had such a positive impact on my life: If I'm stressed, I immediately go and cuddle her, and my stress melts away. She gives my life meaning and purpose because I'm focused on doing what is best for her. I now look at that season as the season I started to live my life outside of myself, not as the awards season I sat out on. Perspective is everything.

Sometimes God doesn't give us certain opportunities so that he can make room for something more. Every season has a purpose, and we need to trust that God will show us the purpose for each season. A phrase a friend of mine shared has stuck with me: "Man's rejection is God's protection" or "Rejection is God's protection." When we go through a breakup or a professional heartbreak or don't get something our heart desires, our reaction is often, "What did I do wrong?" or, "How could I have been better?" The truth is that God likely has a bigger plan for this season of your life. It might not be easy to see right now, and you will probably shed some tears, but trusting in God's reason for each season helps create the Sunshine Mind.

THE SUNSHINE MIND WAY TO . . . THRIVE IN YOUR CURRENT SEASON

IF YOU LOST A JOB, maybe this is an opportunity to start your passion project.

IF YOU ARE HAVING TROUBLE GETTING PREGNANT, maybe this is your season to research and mentally prepare yourself as much as possible.

IF YOU GOT DUMPED, maybe this is your season to focus on who you are and what makes you happy. Maybe focus on creating financial stability.

IF YOU LOST A LOVED ONE, maybe this is your season to honor their memory and reconnect with family. Maybe this is your season to be in community with others who are grieving a loss. Maybe this is your season to start a foundation to bring awareness to any of the reasons you experienced loss.

IF YOU LOST A GAME, maybe this is your season to put your head down and work hard. Maybe the next win will be sweeter because you'll know you've earned it.

SOAK IN THE SUNSHINE

Generations come and generations go,
but the earth remains forever.
The sun rises and the sun sets,
and hurries back to where it rises.

—ECCLESIASTES 1:4-5

Raquelle

As I'm a natural born optimist, soaking in the sun has always come easily to me, but as I've gotten older, I've found that I have to fight more for the sunshine in life. I think it's important for everybody but especially younger people to understand that we live in a world where circumstances can dim our light if we don't continually fight for it. I use a word as strong as *fight* because we must come against the darkness and the hard circumstances that come our way. We do this by soaking in all that's good. The world is beautiful and amazing, and there is far more good than bad. Recently I was in Egypt and was in awe of everything I saw. I specifically remember seeing the Great Sphinx of Giza, and the sun was shining directly on it. I was truly in awe of the ancient Egyptians and that what they built still stands thousands of years later. Experiences like that remind me of God's greatness, and I want to soak in as much of it as I can. It doesn't take going all the way to Egypt. We can find it in nature, the majesty of a beautiful tree, the vastness of the ocean—the sunshine is all around.

The sun has been referenced many times as the glorious lamp of heaven. What a gift God gave us in the sun! Every single day it rises and sets, and it never gets old. One of my (Raquelle speaking) favorite things to do is to go for a walk around the time the sun is setting, with headphones on, listening to worship music with the sun beaming down on my face. I sometimes close my eyes and let the sunshine and music fill my soul with warmth and peace. Take time to connect with the sunlight—and with the Creator—today.

THE SUNSHINE MIND WAY TO . . . SOAK IN THE SUNSHINE

Take time to connect with sunlight today. (Hopefully the weather is good where you live!) Bask in its warmth and be mindful of the feeling you have when it touches your skin. Maintaining your connection to the sun is important. Its benefits include improving your sleep, reducing stress, strengthening your immune system, and boosting your mood. As you take time to soak in the sunshine, be reminded of God's light and love shining on you. Oh, and be sure to wear sunscreen.

WALK CAREFULLY

Be very careful, then, how you
live—not as unwise but as wise.

—EPHESIANS 5:15

Raquelle

Every day, we are faced with opportunities to make choices. I know that when things are going well for me, it's pretty easy to make wise choices. But I think we are tested most when things aren't going well. When times are tough, it can be tempting to turn to things or behaviors that only make things worse in the long run and aren't in our best interest. When we face those moments when we want to make a decision we know isn't wise, that's when prayer can be a powerful tool to come against the situation we are in and help us to choose wisely when we are struggling. When I have been tempted to make a choice that doesn't lead to wisdom, prayer and pausing to reflect on the choice I really want to make have been an anchor, helping me to make a good decision instead of a bad one.

Your "walk" is how you live your life. The Bible calls us to look carefully at our spiritual walk. Ephesians 5:15 encourages us to be wise on our journey. Instinctively, we all know what is right and wrong, good and bad. But as human beings, we all face temptations and obstacles that sometimes get in the way of living a life of wisdom. Living a life of wisdom is possible for all of us when we keep Christ at the center of our lives.

THE SUNSHINE MIND WAY TO . . . WALK CAREFULLY

The biggest tip we have for making wise choices is to pay attention to how you feel afterward. This can apply to behavior choices, friendship choices, career choices—the list goes on. If you feel at peace, that often means you've made a wise choice. If you don't, that's a sign that maybe you didn't. Walking carefully is a lifelong commitment and requires us to check in with the God-given conscience we all have that tells us if something feels good or feels off. We aren't going to make the right choices all the time because we're human, but paying attention to what gives us inner peace is the path to a wise life.

SHAKE IT OFF

Create in me a clean heart, O God,
and renew a right spirit within me.

–PSALM 51:10 ESV

Raquelle

I consistently pray Psalm 51:10 over my life because how we treat others and the energy we bring into our homes and every other space we enter are so important. When it comes to our work, we sometimes face frustrating days. Whether it be working with difficult personalities or having a project go wrong, it's important to keep ourselves in check and keep our spirits right. When I have a challenging day, I have to take a deep breath and look at things from a 360-degree perspective to respond in a way that is helpful and not harmful. Even when responding in a way that is helpful, I often find that the adrenaline of a frustrating situation or negativity can still affect how I feel afterward, so I have to make a conscious effort to wind down on the commute home. If what happened during the day is something I feel I still need to process, I call my trusted friend Ashley, talk it out with her, put some worship music on, and then I shake it off.

o you ever find yourself bringing your work drama into your home life? Do you retreat to your living space with the weight of the day still resting on your shoulders? Do you discuss work events over dinner and then pore over emails before bed? We've come to a place where there is no division between work and home—it all blends together. Sometimes we come home after a frustrating or stressful day and we take it out on the ones we love most. It's easy to do. But this isn't the way of the Sunshine Mind. Your home should be your safe space, your comfort, your joy. If you bring the negativity and stresses from work home, you have no safe haven. As Taylor Swift says, you gotta shake it off, baby! And in this case, do it before you get home to your happy place.

THE SUNSHINE MIND WAY TO . . . SHAKE IT OFF

Put a mason jar by your front door. If anything from your workday is stressing you out, write down what's bothering you and put it in the jar. At the end of each week, burn whatever is inside that jar. (You can also rip it into tiny pieces and throw it away—whatever your demo of choice is.)

A prayer for shaking it off:

Lord,
I pray this Scripture over my situation right now: "Create in me a clean heart, O God, and renew a right spirit within me." Instead of being overwhelmed by anything that has been negative or hard today, I pray that you would renew my spirit and fill it with your goodness and kindness instead. Amen.

REPENT AND RELEASE

If my people who are called by my name humble themselves, and pray and seek my face and turn from their wicked ways, then I will hear from heaven and will forgive their sin and heal their land.

—2 CHRONICLES 7:14 ESV

Raquelle

As a child, I never liked the word *repent*. Because I grew up in church, it was a trigger word for me. Repenting meant I had been bad and was going to get in trouble. But today, to me, to repent means to release. And with the wisdom I now carry, I understand that God will always forgive me when, like letting go of a balloon, I let go of whatever I feel ashamed of. For instance, when I was younger and kept something from my parents, I always felt a huge relief when I eventually told them what I'd done. That's not to say they were proud of me when I snuck out of the house (but I was proud they hadn't caught me—just kidding), but I felt better with them knowing. The feeling of not telling them was more unbearable than admitting my wrongdoings. Repenting can be hard, but once you do it, you feel the release and are brought closer to joy and happiness.

The point of repenting is to return to experiencing life to the fullest. When we need to repent, it's because we've made a decision that's not helpful or best for our life. Just as I felt release when my parents were aware of something wrong I had done, I also feel release when I go to God and repent. When we repent to God, he heals our wounds so we can start fresh. Repentance is a lifelong journey, as we never get everything right all the time, but the more that repenting becomes a practice, the more we experience God's grace and love and can live in the fullness and freedom that brings.

THE SUNSHINE MIND WAY TO . . . REPENT AND RELEASE

If you're having a hard time forgiving yourself, here's a prayer to help you move forward and heal.

Lord,
I come to you humbly to express [insert thing you are repenting of]. I thank you that you hear me and that you forgive me; now I release any feeling of guilt and [insert anything else you may be feeling that's hard]. I pray that you would heal me and help me to make better decisions moving forward that are part of your amazing plan for my life. Amen.

FOLLOW THE SUN

A heart at peace gives life to the body,
but envy rots the bones.

—PROVERBS 14:30

Tanya

Social media. Love it? Hate it? Whatever your relationship with social media, one thing is true—it's here to stay. What a beautiful thing social media can be. It's a way to connect us all, a big platform to create community. And yet it can make us feel the exact opposite—alone and behind. I've had discussions with social media influencers on my podcast, and one thing about their job stands out to me. An influencer is given free products and sent to places and events. Their job is to sell us on these products, places, and events. The images they post are completely set up. Even if they went to Coachella and had a blast, the picture they posted in front of the Ferris wheel was two seconds of their entire weekend. We once had an influencer on our podcast who explained that, yes, she posted an adorable picture of herself and her boyfriend frolicking through a field holding hands, but they did it for the Gram. They don't normally frolic, let alone through a field hand in hand. But looking at that photo from the outside, we may think, "My relationship isn't as great as theirs because we aren't frolicking through fields together." Truly, neither are they!

It's hard not to compare our lives with what we see on social media. Nevertheless, it's important not to. We see countless people having fun on a vacation or at a festival or concert and think, "Why am I not there?" We see everyone looking flawless in a bikini and wonder, "Why don't I look like that?" Well, basically everyone edits their pictures, and most of those bodies aren't real, but that's a whole other story. There is content being circulated that can make you feel left out or less than. But how it affects you is up to you. Every time you pick up your phone to scroll through your social media feed, remember that what you're seeing is a highlight reel. This isn't limited to influencers either. The majority of people only post the positive aspects of their lives, making it seem like their lives are perfect. You don't need to be envious because it's not real. We are fans of the movement happening now that encourages people to be more real on social media by not using filters, pointing out their pimples and stretch marks, and posting their truth.

THE SUNSHINE MIND WAY TO . . . FOLLOW THE SUN

Follow people you admire on social media, people who spread positivity, joy, and light. Follow accounts for their substance instead of for their unrealistic images. Fill your feed with images and words that fill you with joy instead of envy.

Today, look through the list of people you follow. Unfollow any handle that makes you feel less than, and replace that feed with ones that add light and value to your social media.

CHANGE
SOMEONE'S DAY

Gracious words are a honeycomb,
sweet to the soul and healing to the bones.

—PROVERBS 16:24

Raquelle

Recently I was on a work call with my friend and producer Chiara, who works with me on my podcast *Giving Back Generation*. I answered the phone the way I always do, but because Chiara and I spend so much time together, she noticed that something in my tone seemed off. She asked me if anything was wrong. There was something wrong, but I hadn't yet expressed it to anyone. She ended up spending a few minutes encouraging me, and her kind words turned my day around. I could have spent the rest of the day dwelling on what was making me sad. Instead, my conversation with Chiara brought healing to my heart and brightened my day.

In this digital age, we spend a lot of time on the phone, whether it's texting, talking, or FaceTiming. And in each of those instances, our words have the power to change someone's day. When I think about Proverbs 16:24 and how it says words can be healing, it makes me realize that God can use us simply through the words we choose. Words are a free gift we can give, and they have the power to bring healing or pain. The more we remind ourselves of this power, the more carefully we can choose our words and the more intentional we can be with noticing people in our day-to-day lives who need to hear kind words from us.

THE SUNSHINE MIND WAY TO . . . CHANGE SOMEONE'S DAY

We like to end every phone call on a loving note we call the Sunshine Goodbye. Forget about plain ol' "buh-bye" or "see ya later." We prefer to sign off with something more uplifting, like, "It was great to hear your voice," or, "Thank you for reaching out— you truly made my day," or, "I appreciate your help" (if you were speaking with a customer service rep). And we end with an "I love you"—if we really mean it. Ending a phone call with encouragement or love or telling someone how much you appreciate them is a small way to send big sunshine vibes!

FiND POWER IN TRUE PARTNERSHiP

Two people are better off than one, for they can help each other succeed.

ECCLESIASTES 4:9 NLT

Tanya

As a society, we focus a lot on self. And boy, do I get it . . . I'm not one to shy away from a solid selfie or a cute solo shot for the Gram. It's all fun and games until this train of thought takes over. God wants us to be in community, to sharpen each other, to be friends with our neighbors. True partnership can be a game changer.

It was only a few years ago when I realized the magic of true partnership and how beautiful of a gift it can be. In my many years of dating, it wasn't until recent years I noticed a pattern. I would always go for men that didn't live in my state. Now, why would a girl who had such a desire in her heart for marriage look for men outside her state, you might ask? This was because subconsciously I didn't want to let anyone in. I was a modern woman pursuing my career full speed ahead. I could do everything on my own. A man would just slow me down, right? (Or so I thought.) It wasn't until my current relationship that I discovered the power and blessing of true partnership.

My entire career was built on teamwork and partnership. The morning radio show is strong and mighty, and it is successful because of the team we have created. We all have different strengths, and when those strengths are working in tandem, magic is born.

My podcast (that had won People's Choice Awards, for goodness' sake) was also a representation of partnership and teamwork, from my bestie cohost to our incredible producers and talent. My entire career was built on learning how to navigate and work as a collective team with the same goal in mind. Why did I not think I could achieve that in my personal life?

My boyfriend has opened my eyes to an entire world of possibilities I never knew before I met him. He has done the opposite of slow me down; he's helped propel me forward in more ways than one. I'm not saying anyone needs a partner to be complete, but I am saying the right person can make a world of difference. He makes all the years I spent searching, the tears over rejection and heartbreak, totally worth it. I want to encourage you to ask God for his divine discernment. The partner you choose to spend your life with is the most important decision you'll ever make. Do not settle.

THE SUNSHINE MIND WAY TO . . . FIND POWER IN TRUE PARTNERSHIP

Here is a prayer if you're still looking for true partnership:

Dear Lord,
I know the desires you have placed in my heart and have faith you will fulfill those desires. I pray that you give me divine discernment as I navigate the dating world. I pray that you open my eyes and open my heart to the partner you have beautifully created for me. I know everything I'm going through has a purpose, and I pray that you watch over and protect the heart of my future partner as well. In Jesus's name. Amen.

Day 96

BE BOLD

The wicked flee when no one pursues,
but the righteous are bold as a lion.

—PROVERBS 28:1 ESV

Tanya

When I'm dating and am "feeling it" with someone (pre-boyfriend, obviously), I let them know. If I want to see them, I make plans. Being bold and courageous in matters of the heart has benefited me in many ways. One: I don't waste my time sitting around waiting for someone to come to me. I'm a go-getter in all other areas of life, so why would I sit on the sidelines when it comes to my dating life? Two: It helps me figure out if someone is into me or not. Three: Games don't work; they mess with our heads. Authenticity always cuts through. I want to encourage you to be bold when it comes to matters of the heart. Speak up for what you want. If you're in a relationship and this doesn't apply to you, encourage your single friends to step up to the plate.

So much of what we are told—and believe—comes from the fairy tales of our youth. (Rapunzel, I'm looking at you, girl!) We're given the message that we are supposed to sit back and "let the man make the first move." Well, we're gonna suggest something pretty bold right now: ask him out! We are modern women, and we go after what we want. That you're here with us now means you have modern-woman energy too. So listen up, and be bold as a lion.

THE SUNSHINE MIND WAY TO . . . BE BOLD.

Have you been scared to get back into the dating world? What can you do to be bold with your heart today? Make today the day you download all the apps and freshen up that dating profile. And we do mean *all* the apps, every single one. Hey, there are a million dating apps for a reason. Why limit yourself to one when you can widen your pool? The more the merrier; it is a numbers game, after all.

- **GO EARLY!** Have dinner plans with friends? Go to the restaurant an hour early and get a drink at the bar solo. Engage with people sitting near you. Even if there aren't any singles around, you never know who you will meet. Maybe you'll meet someone who has a single nephew or niece, or a single teacher they love, or a single sibling. You never know unless you try.
- **BE PROACTIVE.** Make some little cards with your phone number written on them for easy distribution. If you see someone who catches your eye at the gym, go for it.
- **SAY YES TO EVERYTHING.** How many times have you turned down an invite because you didn't want to go somewhere alone? Let me help you get out of your own way—say yes to everything. Every daily adventure, every new outing, every experience is a chance to meet someone new, so start creating more opportunities for you to shine like the bright sunshine you are!

BE FEARLESS

Light, space, zest—
that's God!
So, with him on my side I'm fearless,
afraid of no one and nothing.

—PSALM 27:1 MSG

Raquelle

I heard a commencement speech that Maria Shriver gave at the University of Michigan. In her speech, she said something that stuck with me. She was talking to the graduating students about the importance of pushing past their fears. She said when leaving college, she wished she had known her fears were more about keeping her small than safe. Graduating college can be a fearful time, as it's a time of transition, a time of the unknown. Maria told the students that graduating college in the day and age we live in, while being the most uncertain of times, is an incredible opportunity because they have been given the gift of a shredded rule book. Much of what used to be considered "normal" has now gone out the window, and this allows room for the students to be creative and not necessarily to repeat their parents' lives or what worked back then. We have the amazing opportunity right now to live bravely and authentically.

We can't express enough the importance of facing your fears so you can live a life of abundance. Often we choose what seems safe and comfortable, or we make decisions based on what our loved ones expect from us rather than going for our own deepest dreams and desires. We let fear get the best of us. Remember that your dreams and desires came from God, so don't let anyone or anything make you feel afraid. Whatever it is that you want—go for it! Don't let fear hold you back.

THE SUNSHINE MIND WAY TO . . . BE FEARLESS

When you find yourself holding back because of fear, pray this prayer:

Dear God,
Thank you for the dreams and desires you have given me. As I pursue these dreams and desires, help me to face my fears head-on, knowing that with you I have nothing to fear. Amen.

EXPERiENCE JOY

The joy of the Lord is your strength.

—NEHEMiAH 8:10

Tanya

The way we approach the mundane things in life has a significant impact on our positive energy. One small thing I do every morning when I walk into the studio is turn on all the lights, flicker them on and off, and shout, "Good morning, everyone!" It sounds silly, and possibly annoying, but it shifts the energy dramatically. (And it literally makes the room brighter!) The way you approach the little, daily things is the way you approach everything in life. Let's bring as much joy to our days as we can.

To experience and share joy is one of the greatest strengths we can have. That's right—joy is a strength. Joy can change an entire atmosphere. It can change your life. It can change someone else's life. No matter your situation or privilege, life can be hard. It's easy to get caught up in the fray and feel the weight of the world on our shoulders, but we should never forget the importance of feeling joy even in the simplest things. Remember when you were a kid and how it felt to swing blissfully at the park or chase after your friends at the playground? We should still be experiencing those same feelings of joy in our adult lives. Our joy comes from the Lord, and it is definitely a strength.

THE SUNSHINE MIND WAY TO . . . EXPERIENCE JOY

Experiencing joy is at the center of the Sunshine Mind. We make fun a priority! With everything we have going on with work and our other responsibilities, it's important to plan for a good time. Walking to grab coffee with a friend? Race to the light! Zooming with your coworkers? Pick a costume theme! Having people over for dinner? Make it a game night! Always make fun—and joy—a priority.

ACCESS THE FRUIT
OF THE SPIRIT

The fruit of the Spirit is love, joy, peace, patience, kindness, goodness, faithfulness, gentleness and self-control. Against such things there is no law.

—GALATIANS 5:22–23 NIV 1984

Raquelle

I could share many stories about the importance of the fruit of the Spirit in my day-to-day life, but one that stands out to me that I'm sure many of you can relate to is when a family member of mine was wronged by a friend of mine. If someone says something about me, I can deal with it, but if they say something about someone I care about, it's harder to handle because I become protective. Can you relate to that feeling? Anyway, this specific situation was something that needed to be addressed if I still wanted to have a good friendship with the person, but how I handled it was important. Instead of going off on my friend and saying hurtful things, I took a few days and made sure I spent time with God so I wouldn't react from an emotional place (a.k.a. I accessed self-control). After that, I was able to speak the truth but in a kind way. My friend ended up apologizing to my family member, and it turns out the situation was a result of a lot of miscommunication. Had I not accessed the fruit of the Spirit, I could have said words I would never have been able to take back. I am so grateful for the Holy Spirit, because when we are filled with the Spirit, that energy naturally flows out of us.

ny time we feel emotions that are the opposite of the fruit of the Spirit, we need to get centered again. You might be thinking, "Well, this all sounds great, but how do I access these fruits?" It's simple: you spend time with God. Sometimes you'll hear people make excuses for their actions: "Oh, well, I just have a temper and I tend to get angry," or, "I'm just wired this way, and self-control isn't really my thing." But that's not true. The power of God can break through anything. And the fruits of the Spirit aren't unique to us or to you; they are available to everyone. If you ask God for these things—love, joy, peace, patience, kindness, goodness, faithfulness, gentleness, and self-control—and you spend time with him, you will be filled with these fruits.

THE SUNSHINE MIND WAY TO . . . ACCESS THE FRUIT OF THE SPIRIT

Spending time with God helps us access the fruit of the Spirit and live out these qualities in our daily lives. But what does spending time with God look like? A lot of things!

- Praying every morning or every evening
- Listening to worship music
- Reading the Bible
- Going for a walk in nature
- Journaling or drawing and reflecting on God's goodness

LiVE OUT THE FRUiT OF THE SPiRIT

The fruit of the Spirit is love, joy, peace, patience, kindness, goodness, faithfulness, gentleness and self-control. Against such things there is no law.

—GALATiANS 5:22-23 NiV 1984

Raquelle

My mom tells the story of a woman in her neighborhood who was always angry. Every time my mom would see her walking her dog, no matter what this woman's mood was, my mom would always smile and say hello. After weeks of my mom doing this, the woman softened and her mood shifted. She stopped my mom one day and said, "You know, no one notices each other anymore. People are always in a hurry—cars speeding by—and it is a shame. But I wanted to say thank you for always smiling and saying hello to me." They ended up having the most beautiful and meaningful conversation. Perhaps this woman had been deeply hurt throughout her life, and through my mom showing her a simple act of kindness with a smile and a wave, she was able to make a connection with another person and feel the love of God.

The fruits of the Spirit are what we experience when we spend time in God's presence and are filled with God's Spirit. They are the goal of how we want to live and show we're really following him. Of course, our natural human tendencies can be opposite of the fruits, but the more we practice the fruits of the Spirit, the more they will become habit and create the most meaningful and loving connections with others.

LOVE

When you experience God's love, you can't help but love other people. It's part of who you are because God is love, and his love in you overflows to others.

JOY

Often people think the spiritual life is heavy or intense, but we've found that the more we are filled up with God, the more we experience joy—and not only a little bit of joy but an abundance of it! We can be going through the toughest of circumstances and still feel joy and even find humor in our daily lives.

PEACE

It is possible to have peace no matter your circumstances. We have been in some of the wildest situations where the natural reaction would have been to feel afraid, but because we know we always carry the peace of God with us, the feeling of peace instantly replaces feelings of fear or worry.

PATIENCE

We think patience is a tough one because it goes against our natural human tendency. We want things *now*, but if you stop and think about it, many of the best things in life take time. Building a good relationship takes time. It can be like growing a plant. It's not like you plant the seed, then water it and—*boom!*—a few seconds later you have a beautiful flower. It's a slow process that requires patience—it may take days, weeks, or even months—but the waiting is worth it to get to that lovely blossom.

KiNDNESS

Kindness is truly one of the best things in the world, and we can all practice it—with friends, with strangers, with anyone at all. It can be as simple as giving someone a smile, or it can be going out of your way to help someone in need. Kindness can come in many forms, but even the smallest act of kindness can be felt deeply.

GOODNESS

Goodness encompasses many things. When you know God, you naturally want to be good—being good to yourself and putting good out into the world. We can live out goodness through our words and our actions, including the way we speak to ourselves and to others.

FAITHFULNESS

Being faithful is important because even when you don't see what's coming next, you can still practice faithfulness to God, knowing that all things are working together for good in God's plan. We know that our end goal is eternity, so no matter what we face in this lifetime, when we are faithful to God, we are good no matter what.

GENTLENESS

We have always loved the concept of gentleness because we believe that when people think of God, they think of strength in the form of a powerful lion. That absolutely *is* God, but we've always loved the idea of God being the lion *and* the lamb. We are meant to be fierce and bold, but we're also meant to be gentle with people, and gentleness is a form of strength. Jesus lived his entire life with gentleness, meeting people where they were. There is boldness in gentleness.

SELF-CONTROL

We all benefit from having self-control, don't we? Any time we have *not* had self-control—for example, eating too much and then feeling sick or reacting badly to a friend who has upset us—we regret it almost immediately. Our actions—eating that extra piece of cake or yelling at our friend—might feel good in the moment. But almost immediately after, we ask ourselves, "Why did I do that?" Self-control is an amazing fruit of the Spirit to have because giving in to our impulses never leads to long-term peace. God wants us to live our lives being able to control ourselves.

CLOSING NOTE

Thank you for spending the last one hundred days with us. Our goal is for you to feel as if you've gained two new best friends you can always come back to if you need a little sunshine. We know life can be tricky and complicated and messy. Our hope is that you approach these situations of adversity with a new mindset—the Sunshine Mind—where our focus is perspective and our approach is solutions-oriented. We pray you look at life with an open mind and an open heart, always leading with love and light. We hope you continue to treat yourself as you do others, with kindness, forgiveness, generosity, and grace. These are the pillars for a joyful life, which we all deserve.

In times of uncertainty or stress, remember God is with you and is always by your side. Come back to this book when you need a reminder, encouragement, or a little sunshine during a stormy season. We're always here for you and can't wait to hear about the good you shine into this world.

With light,

Tanya and Raquelle

NOTES

1. Maya Angelou in "Oprah Talks to Maya Angelou," Oprah.com, original article appeared December 2000 issue of *O, The Oprah Magazine*, https://www.oprah.com/omagazine/oprah-interviews-maya-angelou/3.
2. *Legally Blonde*, directed by Robert Luketic, performance by Reese Witherspoon (Paramount, 2001).
3. Joyce Meyer, *Eight Ways to Keep the Devil under Your Feet* (New York: Hachette, 2002), 87.
4. Dr. Seuss, *I Can Read with My Eyes Shut!* (New York: Random House, 1978).
5. *Oprah's Master Class*, episode 102, "Condoleezza Rice," aired February 13, 2011, on OWN, 18:38, https://www.youtube.com/watch?v=uQgHsm5cc2c.
6. *Oprah's Master Class*, Dr. Maya Angelou: "Love Liberates," aired January 16, 2011, on OWN, https://www.youtube.com/watch?v=d7dxnQQEpXs.
7. Helen Howarth Lemmel, "Turn Your Eyes upon Jesus," https://hymnary .org/text/o_soul_are_you_weary_and_troubled.
8. Aired April 16, 2018, https://podcasts.apple.com/us/podcast/ep-30 -breaking-wind-breaking-away/id1279955329?i=1000409033048.
9. *The Works of William Law*, vol. 7, 1893, 74.

From the Publisher

GREAT BOOKS

ARE EVEN BETTER WHEN THEY'RE SHARED!

Help other readers find this one:

- Post a review at your favorite online bookseller

- Post a picture on a social media account and share why you enjoyed it

- Send a note to a friend who would also love it—or better yet, give them a copy

Thanks for reading!